CONTEMPORARY'S

WORK-WISE
Tactics for Job Success

Project Editor
Frances A. Wiser

Consultant
Carol Molek
Adult Education Coordinator
Tuscarora Intermediate Unit
Adult Education and Job Training Center
Lewistown, Pennsylvania

Developed by
Contemporary Books, Inc.
and
Visual Education Corporation
Princeton, New Jersey

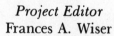

CB
CONTEMPORARY
BOOKS
CHICAGO

Cover photo: © Michael Slaughter, courtesy of the Compri Hotel, Schaumburg, Illinois
Pages 1, 4, 12, 23, 36, 42, 47, 67, 68, 80, 93, 101, 104, 115: Robert Bruschini/Studio B; pages 53, 57, 89, 109: Gary Mattie; page 116: New York University, Luigi Pellettieri; page 82: Visual Education Corporation

Published by Contemporary Books, Inc.
180 North Michigan Avenue, Chicago, Illinois 60601
Manufactured in the United States of America
International Standard Book Number 0-8092-4100-5

Published simultaneously in Canada by
Fitzhenry & Whiteside
195 Allstate Parkway
Valleywood Business Park
Markham, Ontario L3R 4T8
Canada

Editorial Director
Caren Van Slyke

Assistant Editorial Director
Mark Boone

Project Editor
Frances A. Wiser

Editor
Suzanne Eckert

Editorial Assistant
Carol Ciaston

Cover Designer
Lois Koehler

Production Consultants
Jean Farley Brown
Norma Fioretti

Reviewers
Kathy Osmus
Betsy Rubin

Writers
Natalie Goldstein
Cheryl Morrison
Karen Theroux

Production Supervisor
Anita Crandall

Designers
Max Crandall
Susan Riley

Illustrator
Bill Colrus

Photo Researcher
Toby Mosko

CONTENTS

GETTING READY FOR INTERVIEWS 36

INTERVIEW DO'S AND DON'TS 47

MAKING THE RIGHT CHOICE 57

INTRODUCTION

Do you know how to go about getting a job? When you get the job you want, will you know how to succeed at it? *Work-Wise: Tactics for Job Success* can help you acquire and develop the skills you need to obtain and hold a job.

Work-Wise is divided into 11 sections. This book can help you no matter what stage of the job-search process you're in.

♦ If you're not sure what kind of work you want to do, Section 1 can help you learn more about your goals and interests.

♦ Sections 2 and 3 explain where and how you can look for a job.

♦ Sections 4 and 5 discuss interviews—how to prepare for them and what to do when you go on them.

♦ Section 6 shows you things to consider in choosing a job that's right for you.

♦ *Work-Wise* can also help you once you have a job. In Sections 7 and 8, you will learn how to adjust to your job as well as how to balance work and family demands. Section 9 deals with your legal rights as an employee.

♦ Finally, Sections 10 and 11 show you ways to move up in your company or to move on to new jobs, when necessary.

Each section of *Work-Wise* begins with a story about a person who has faced and solved a job-related problem. The content of each section is designed to help you learn job skills and then to provide you with the opportunity to practice using these skills. For example, in Section 3, you will learn how to write an application letter for a job. Then, in the same section, you will have the chance to actually write one.

Within each section, words that you may need to learn are shown in a **darker type**. At the end of each section, you will have a chance to apply what you have learned in four different types of exercises. Many of these exercises ask you to put yourself in someone else's place to answer questions or solve a problem. That way, you learn how to respond in situations that may occur in your own job search.

There is an answer key at the end of this book for exercises that have specific, correct answers. However, many of the questions and exercises are based on your personal experiences, ideas, and opinions. Of course, there are no answer key references for those questions.

We hope that *Work-Wise* will help you to better understand your interests and abilities and to make the most of yourself in today's job market.

SECTION 1

TAKING STOCK OF YOURSELF

Carlos lives in a large city near a job training center that places job hunters. When Carlos made an appointment at the center, he didn't know what to expect. His friend had suggested that Carlos see a job counselor. And now that he and Ms. Chin were sitting together and talking, he was glad he had followed his friend's advice.

"The best way to begin," Ms. Chin said, "is to think about what you like to do. Have you ever had a job that you liked?"

"Yes, a few years ago I worked as a deliveryman for a pizza shop. I liked that job pretty well," Carlos said.

"What part of the job did you like the best?" Ms. Chin asked.

"I really liked driving the van," Carlos replied. "I don't think I could ever sit behind a desk all day."

"Was there anything you didn't like about the job?" she asked.

"Yes," he said. "I missed working with people. I spent most of my time alone in the van."

"It seems to me that you might enjoy a job that involves both driving and dealing with people," Ms. Chin said.

"Yes, that sounds good," Carlos replied. "But how many jobs are there where I can do that?"

"Oh, there are quite a few," Ms. Chin said. "You could drive a school bus or a city bus. Or you could drive a van for senior citizens or the disabled."

"Where do I go to find out more about these jobs?" Carlos asked.

"You're already there," Ms. Chin said with a smile. "I can give you plenty of information about these jobs. But first, I think we need to zero in on the kinds of things that interest you most and the skills that you perform best. I like to call it 'taking stock of yourself.'"

Knowing Yourself

When Carlos met with Ms. Chin, she asked him questions about his likes and dislikes. She wanted to know how he liked to spend his time and what his talents and skills were. She also asked what mattered most to him about his job and what his work experience was. His answers helped him realize what was important to him in a job.

In much the same way, you will answer questions throughout this section. You will use the answers to learn more about yourself and about the kinds of jobs that are right for you. There are no right or wrong answers to the questions in this section. And no one else needs to know your answers.

When you answer the questions, be honest about yourself. Your answers will tell you what's important to you and which kinds of jobs may be best for you.

Your Interests

Let's start with questions about your interests. Your **interests** are the activities that you enjoy and the things you like to talk about or read about. You are more likely to enjoy your work if it involves a subject or an activity you're interested in.

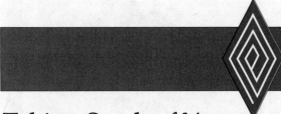

Taking Stock of Your Interests

Your responses to the items listed below will help you identify your interests. After each statement, write *yes* if it applies to you or *no* if it does not.

1. I like working with my hands. _____

2. I enjoy spending time outdoors. _____

3. I like working with machinery. _____

4. I enjoy solving puzzles. _____

5. I like using my head to solve problems. _____

6. I enjoy traveling. _____

7. I like working with numbers. _____

Your Values

The features of a job that are most important to you reflect your **work values**. These features may include the work environment, level of physical activity, wages, and so on. For instance, some people can't concentrate or do their jobs well in a noisy office. Others think that noise and excitement make an office stimulating. You should consider these and many other work values when you look for a job.

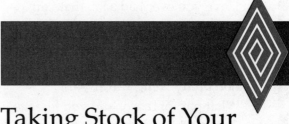

Taking Stock of Your Values

Your responses to the items listed below will help you identify your work values. After each statement, write *yes* if it applies to you or *no* if it does not.

1. I like doing the same thing over and over. _____

2. I like to spend a lot of time with other people. _____

3. I enjoy helping other people. _____

4. I like physical activity. _____

5. I prefer to follow directions rather than to figure out what to do by myself. _____

6. I enjoy challenges._____

7. Job security is extremely important to me.

_____

8. I work best in a quiet, peaceful atmosphere.

_____

Listing Your Assets

Understanding your interests and values can help you decide what you want from a job. But you also need to figure out what you have to offer. Every person has **assets** to offer an employer. Your assets can be grouped in the following categories:

♦ **aptitudes and talents**
♦ **basic skills**
♦ **technical skills**
♦ **background skills**
♦ **education and training**

Aptitudes are natural abilities that people have. Aptitudes that you have and can perform without much difficulty are **talents**. For example, if you are good at fixing things, then it isn't hard for you to learn to fix things you're not familiar with. When you identify your talents, you can figure out which things you can learn most easily.

Skills are abilities that usually require learning and practice. Repairing a car, for example, takes skill. No matter how much talent you have, you can't repair a car unless you have learned this skill through training and experience.

Most employers expect you to have certain **basic skills** before they hire you. For example, applicants for any sales job would be expected to know how to add and subtract. Other important basic skills include reading and writing.

You probably have more skills than you realize. When people list their skills, they often list only their basic skills or their **technical skills**. Typing is a technical skill, and so is

operating a cash register or a forklift. But most adults also have **background skills.** These are skills that you use in many areas of your life that can also help you on the job. Helping people to solve problems is a background skill. Organizing people or information is a background skill, too.

All of your skills can be used as **qualifications** for jobs. For example, if you have good driving skills and first aid training, you might use them to help you qualify for a job as an ambulance driver.

Education and training can help you get the skills and knowledge you need for certain jobs. That's why diplomas and certificates are accepted as proof of your most important qualifications.

The next list of questions will help you identify your talents, skills, education, and training. Being able to identify certain skills as strengths is a good way to gain the confidence you need for the job search. Your answers to the following questions will help you figure out what kinds of jobs you are likely to do well.

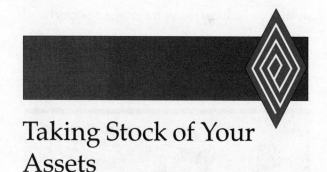

Taking Stock of Your Assets

Make a list of five tasks that you perform in a day at home or on the job. Include tasks such as cooking, taking care of children, making repairs, and dealing with people.

1. _____

2. _____

3. _____

4. _____

5. _____

Talents

Which of these tasks do you think you are especially good at? These are some of your talents.

_____

_____

_____

Skills

Which of these tasks require technical skills? Include tasks such as using a computer or operating machinery.

_____

_____

Which of these tasks require background skills? Include tasks such as keeping track of details or speaking more than one language.

_____

_____

_____

Education and Training

Which of these tasks required you to get additional education or training to perform?

_____

_____

_____

Caring for others is valuable experience that this mother can transfer to the workplace.

Which One Appeals Most to You?

Jobs usually focus on a particular type of work task. Work tasks have four main focuses:

♦ **Data**. Some jobs focus heavily on **data**, or information, such as facts, numbers, papers, and files. Book-keepers and secretaries work with data; so do bank tellers and data entry clerks.

♦ **Ideas**. Some jobs put heavy emphasis on finding new ways to express ideas or solve problems. People in these jobs include artists, writers, performers, and scientists.

♦ **People**. Helping, teaching, and caring for people is the focus of some jobs, including nursing, teaching, and sales.

♦ **Things**. Some workers spend most of their time with machines, tools, or materials. People who do this include carpenters and cooks.

Most jobs involve some of each of these work tasks. For example, most secretarial tasks involve working with data, but secretaries also work with people. Secretaries may also work with ideas (to solve problems) and with things (such as dictation machines, computers, or typewriters). Even though jobs such as this one involve many work tasks, most jobs still focus on one work task. Finding out which work tasks you prefer can help you identify jobs that you may enjoy.

Your Work Experience

When you try to convince an employer that you can do a job, the best proof you can offer is past work experience. In fact, any work experience you have may help you in your job search.

Your work experience includes jobs in traditional settings, such as stores, offices, and factories. It also includes work you have done in private homes. For example, if you have earned money cleaning houses, caring for children, or mowing lawns, that, too, is part of your work experience. Work as a homemaker involves a wide variety of skills and abilities that can be turned into work experience when you seek a job. Volunteer work, such as distributing food to the homeless, is also work experience.

Your work experience tells an employer what kinds of skills you have used in jobs. Employers often require specific work experience as a qualification for jobs. For example, you may need to get work experience in retail sales to qualify for a job as a salesperson in a department store.

By reviewing your own work experience, you can identify qualifications that can help you get certain jobs. You can also learn about the kinds of work you enjoy. Ms. Chin helped Carlos do this by asking him questions about jobs he had held. Use the list of questions that follow to help you do this.

Taking Stock of Your Work Experience

List four jobs you have held, including traditional jobs, work in private homes, and volunteer work. For each job, you will identify the focus of the work tasks you performed. Place a check mark in the correct column for each job. (Each job may have more than one

work task, so you can check more than one column, if necessary.) Then, on the lines below, write what you liked and disliked about each job.

For example, Carlos might fill out his list this way:

Job	Data	Ideas	People	Things
Delivering pizza				✓

What did I like about this job?
Driving the van, not sitting behind a desk.
What did I dislike about this job?
I missed working with people.

Job	Data	Ideas	People	Things

What did I like about this job?

What did I dislike about this job?

Job	Data	Ideas	People	Things

What did I like about this job?

What did I dislike about this job?

Job	Data	Ideas	People	Things

What did I like about this job?

What did I dislike about this job?

Job	Data	Ideas	People	Things

What did I like about this job?

_____

_____

What did I dislike about this job?

_____

_____

Of all the jobs you listed, which job did you like most? Why?

_____

_____

Of all the jobs you listed, which did you dislike the most? Why?

_____

_____

Of all the jobs you listed, which job did you do the best? Why?

_____

_____

Deciding Which Jobs Are Right for You

Throughout this section, you have answered questions about interests, values, assets, and work experience. How do you put all of this information together to identify the kinds of jobs you should look for?

First, look over the answers about your work experience. On the jobs you liked most, did you work mainly with people, ideas, things, or data?

_____

When you review what you liked and disliked about each of the jobs you have held, you will probably see a pattern. For example, you may notice that you preferred jobs where you spent time alone outdoors. Or you may find that what you enjoyed most about jobs was solving problems or helping people. Is there a pattern? If so, what is it?

_____

_____

Next, review what you wrote about your assets on page 4. What skills and educational qualifications did you list that you could offer an employer?

_____

_____

_____

_____

What other job skills and training interest you?

_____

_____

Review your answers about your interests and values. This will help you get a clearer picture of yourself.

Now think about some specific jobs that interest you. Consider jobs you know about already. They might be jobs you have done, jobs done by people you know, or jobs that you have seen other people doing. You can also learn about other kinds of jobs by looking at the help-wanted advertisements in your local newspaper.

Two other sources of job information are reference books you can find in most public libraries: the *Occupational Outlook Handbook* and the *Dictionary of Occupational Titles*. These books are both published by the U.S. Department of Labor. The *Occupational Outlook Handbook* gives detailed descriptions of more than 200 jobs and brief descriptions of 200 others. Each job description includes information about what workers do on the job, working conditions, training requirements, and other important information. The *Dictionary of Occupational Titles* lists 20,000 occupations and gives a definition of each one. It tells what tasks are performed by people in that occupation.

My Job Interests

On a separate sheet of paper, copy the four columns below. You will list three jobs that interest you. After the job title, write about the primary work tasks, skills you need to have, and educational qualifications. If you don't know this information, check with people who know about the job, help-wanted ads, the *Occupational Outlook Handbook*, or the *Dictionary of Occupational Titles*.

Job Title	Work Tasks	Skills You Need	Education
1. _____	_____	_____	_____
_____	_____	_____	_____
2. _____	_____	_____	_____
_____	_____	_____	_____
3. _____	_____	_____	_____
_____	_____	_____	_____

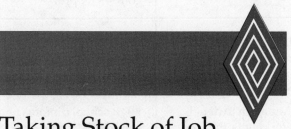

Taking Stock of Job Possibilities

When you have learned about a few jobs, you can answer the following questions. Your answers will help you identify which jobs you should consider pursuing.

1. Of all these jobs, which ones involve activities or subjects that interest you?

_____

_____

2. Which of the jobs would provide the job features you value most?

_____

3. Which jobs would make the best use of your talents, skills, and training?

_____

_____

4. Which of the jobs do you have the most work experience for?

_____

_____

One or more of the jobs probably appeared in a few of your answers above. Those jobs are probably the ones that are best for you. They match your preferences and qualifications. Now consider these jobs in terms of practical needs, such as where a job is located, what hours you would work, and how much money you would make.

Are You New to the Job Market?

If this is your first time looking for a job, there are a few details you may need to take care of first. One important detail is to get a Social Security card. The Social Security Administration assigns you a Social Security number, which is printed on your Social Security card.

All workers must have a Social Security number. You need your number in order to fill out job applications, enroll in schools, and file your income tax returns. Any people, such as your children, who are listed as

A SAMPLING OF JOBS

The chart below includes nine jobs and gives details about them.

OCCUPATION	WORK TASK	ABILITIES	QUALIFICATIONS
Auto Body Repairers	Things	Using hand tools, having physical strength	High school diploma preferred but not necessary; a certificate from a trade school is helpful
Cook or Kitchen Helper	Things	Cooking, working quickly, doing several activities at once	Entry-level jobs have no education requirement, but people with high school diplomas and post–high school training are most likely to advance
Corrections Officer	People	Giving instruction, helping people solve problems	High school diploma, additional training in psychology or related fields preferred
Counter Clerk	People	Taking customer orders, making change, working a cash register	High school diploma preferred but not required
Florist	Ideas	Flair for color and design	High school diploma preferred
Photographer	Ideas	Artistic ability, patience, accuracy and attention to detail	High school diploma preferred but not required, photography courses helpful
Paramedic	People	Using medical equipment, handling stress	High school diploma, training in emergency care
Statistical Clerk	Data	Attention to detail, working with numbers, using a computer keyboard	High school diploma; courses in typing, data processing, and bookkeeping are helpful
Typist/Word Processor	Data	Using a typewriter or computer keyboard, accuracy, attention to detail, good spelling and grammar	High school graduate

dependents on your income tax returns, must also have Social Security numbers.

When you have a job, both you and your employer pay into the Social Security fund each month. This fund entitles you to certain benefits, such as money after retirement. The government uses your Social Security number to determine when you should get your benefits.

To get a Social Security card, go to a Social Security office and ask for an application form. To locate the office nearest you, look in the phone book under United States Government, then under the subheading Social Security.

Social Security cards are free, but you must fill out an application form to get one. You also must provide two documents that prove your age, citizenship, and identity. Most people use their birth certificates and one other form of identification, such as a driver's license, medical records, or school records. If you can't get an official copy of your birth certificate, you can use some other record of your birth that was made before you were five years old. This could be a record from a hospital or religious organization. These documents must be original documents or official copies, not photocopies.

On the application, you must write your full name, your address, your sex, the date and place of your birth, and your parents' names. You must also say whether you are a citizen of the United States or a resident alien. If you are not a U.S. citizen or a resident alien, you must attach a statement to your application that explains your status and tells why you need a Social Security number. On the application, information on race and ethnic description is voluntary.

You will be given two Social Security cards—one to carry with you at all times and one to keep in a safe place. If you lose both cards and you know your number, you can obtain replacements from the Social Security office.

You need to have a Social Security card to work in the United States.

Do You Need Working Papers?

In addition to a Social Security card, you may need to get some other documents before you look for a job. You will need to do this if you are younger than the legal employment age in your state or if you are not a United States citizen.

If you are younger than 18, call your state's Department of Labor to learn about your state's child labor laws. Do this before you begin looking for jobs. In most states, you must be at least 16 or 18 years old to hold a full-time job legally. If you are younger than the minimum age, you must obtain a work permit to have a job.

No matter how old you are, you can accept part-time jobs, such as babysitting or painting in private homes. However, if you haven't reached your state's legal working age, you need a work permit before you can accept a job with a business. With a work permit, you can get a part-time job in a hospital, on a farm, or at a gas station, store, or other retail business. According to the U.S. Department of Labor, 5 million people between the ages of 14 and 18 hold jobs at some time during the year.

Anyone who works in the United States must be a citizen of this country or must provide documentation that says he or she has

QUESTIONS ON A SOCIAL SECURITY CARD APPLICATION

3 CITIZENSHIP
(Check One)

☐ U. S. Citizen ☐ Legal Alien Allowed To Work ☐ Legal Alien Not Allowed To Work ☐ Foreign Student Allowed Restricted Employment ☐ Conditionally Legalized Alien Allowed To Work ☐ Other (See Instructions On Page 2)

4 SEX

☐ Male ☐ Female

5 RACE/ETHNIC DESCRIPTION
(Check One Only—Voluntary)

☐ Asian, Asian-American Or Pacific Islander ☐ Hispanic ☐ Black (Not Hispanic) ☐ North American Indian Or Alaskan Native ☐ White (Not Hispanic)

6 DATE OF BIRTH _____
MONTH DAY YEAR

7 PLACE OF BIRTH _____ CITY STATE OR FOREIGN COUNTRY FCI
(Do Not Abbreviate)

Office Use Only

8 MOTHER'S MAIDEN NAME _____
FIRST FULL MIDDLE NAME LAST NAME AT HER BIRTH

9 FATHER'S NAME _____
FIRST FULL MIDDLE NAME LAST

The questions above were taken from an application for a Social Security card. Do you know the answers to all of the questions?

the legal right to work in this country. This documentation varies, depending on the background, status, and skills of the alien. Aliens usually get these documents before they come to the United States.

If you are not a citizen, be sure to take one of these documents with you when you meet with an employer. All employers are required by law to check these documents. If you don't have one of these documents, contact the Immigration and Naturalization Service.

Points to Remember

In this section you learned that there are many ways of finding out what kinds of jobs are right for you. Some of the most important suggestions include these:

♦ learn about your interests and work values
♦ know your assets
♦ evaluate your past work experience
♦ understand the focus of certain jobs

Word-Wise

Fill in the blanks below to complete the sentences. The answers are key terms introduced in this section.

1. Your _____ are the skills and talents that make you attractive to employers.

2. Activities that you enjoy are your
_____ .

3. Some _____ _____
are reading, writing, and doing math.

4. _____ _____
are the features of a job that are important to you.

Putting It to Work

A friend is looking for a new job. Your friend doesn't know exactly what type of work she wants, and she has come to you for advice. Make a list of five questions you would ask your friend to help her identify the type of work she would like.

1. _____
2. _____
3. _____
4. _____
5. _____

You Be the Judge

Suppose you are having trouble deciding what type of work you are interested in. You have talked with a friend who suggested that you see a job placement counselor. Another friend said that seeing a counselor was a waste of time for him because he couldn't get the job he wanted. What would you do? Why?

_____
_____
_____
_____
_____
_____

Getting the Facts

Imagine that you can choose any job that you want. Use the sources discussed in this section to learn about a job that you think you would like. Then use the sources to find answers to the following questions.

1. What job did you choose?

_____

2. What are some of the duties performed?

_____
_____

3. What are the usual working hours?

_____

4. What educational qualifications are required? _____

_____

5. About how many jobs of this type are available? _____

_____

6. What is the job outlook? _____

_____

7. Are there opportunities for advancement?

_____

If so, what are they? _____

_____

8. Do you still think you would like this job?

_____

Why or why not? _____

_____

WEIGHING YOUR OPTIONS

Joan Waters and her cousin Sandy were drinking coffee and talking in Joan's kitchen. "Now that Michael and Jessica are both in school, I need to get a job," Joan said. "I'm hoping to get a job as a waitress, but I haven't seen anything in the paper that's close enough to my apartment."

"Did you ever meet my friend Kim?" Sandy asked.

"Sure. We met at the party you had last year."

"I was just talking to her yesterday. She complained that two of the wait-

resses at the steakhouse that she manages quit without giving notice. Kim had to ask the other waitresses to work double shifts until she could find replacements. I'll bet at least one of those jobs is still open."

"Where is the steakhouse?" Joan asked.

"It's on Wilmot near State Street. It's called Monte's Steakhouse," Sandy said.

"That's great. I could even walk there," Joan said. "Do you think I should call her or stop by?"

"I'd call her to see if the job's still available," Sandy said.

"I forgot her last name," Joan said.

"It's Vaughn," Sandy said, as Joan got out a pen and paper to write it down. "When you call, mention my name, and tell Kim that I suggested that you call her."

Joan smiled. "Thanks," she said. "I'll call her today after the lunch hour rush."

"Let me know what happens. If there's anything else I can do, give me a call."

"You've already helped a lot just by telling me about this," Joan said. "Thanks again."

"No problem," Sandy said smiling. "If it works out, you'll just owe me a free steak dinner."

Networking with Family and Friends

Sandy gave Joan one lead for finding a job. Using personal contacts in this way is called **networking**. This means that you use your network of friends, relatives, and acquaintances to help you find work. The people in your network may not be able to offer you a job. But they may be able to tell you about others who can.

Many employers use networking, too. They hope to find reliable workers by getting recommendations from employees, clients, and suppliers. So networking can tip you off to jobs that haven't been advertised. Finding out about unadvertised jobs is a very important method that is often overlooked. These kinds of jobs are described as "hidden jobs," and networking is how most people find them.

You can start networking by telling your friends and relatives that you're looking for a job. Then tell everyone you know—former employers, neighbors, and people in your community. The more people you include in your network, the more likely you are to get the job leads you want. Even the most casual acquaintance may have helpful information to give you.

Joan, for example, got suggestions from several friends and neighbors in addition to Sandy. "I saw a help-wanted sign in the window at Bennie's Burgers yesterday," Joan's next-door neighbor told her.

When friends, neighbors, or acquaintances tell you about job openings, ask them if you may mention their names to employers. Mentioning the name of someone an employer already knows may help you get an appointment. On the other hand, friends who know little about your work performance may not want you to use their names.

You can also use networking to gather information about jobs *before* you actually apply. For example, Joan's sister-in-law,

Millie, works as a sales clerk in a department store. If Joan were interested in working in sales, she might ask Millie to describe the details of her job.

Who Can You Include in Your Network?

Always keep a record of the contacts you make when networking. Keep a notebook in which you can write the job lead and the name of the person who gave it to you.

In the blank spaces that follow, write the names of four people you might want to tell about your job search. Then explain how each person might be able to help you. An example is provided for you.

Name	How This Person Can Help
Example:	
Fernando Nieves	May know of openings in his company.
1. _____	_____
	_____
2. _____	_____
	_____
3. _____	_____
	_____
4. _____	_____
	_____

Responding to Help-Wanted Signs

Have you ever noticed help-wanted signs in windows? This is a common way for many restaurants, shops, and other small businesses to advertise job openings.

Some employers advertise by placing help-wanted signs on bulletin boards. You can usually find bulletin boards in the following places:

- **supermarkets**
- **shopping centers**
- **post offices**
- **community centers**
- **government buildings, such as City Hall**

Read the help-wanted sign carefully before you call or visit the employer. If the sign includes a telephone number, write it down, then call for an appointment. If there is no phone number on the sign, you can visit without an appointment.

If you decide to drop in on an employer, make sure you are dressed appropriately for the job. Also, be prepared for an **interview**. Be ready to answer questions about your education and job experience, and be prepared to fill out an application form. You will read more about interviews and application forms in Sections 3, 4, and 5.

Should You Drop In?

The impression you make when you drop in on an employer can help you get a job. Ask yourself these questions when you see a help-wanted sign:

- Am I dressed well enough to go in and ask for a job?
- Can I remember enough personal information to fill out an application form?
- Will I miss this opportunity if I wait?
- If I don't want to drop in now, how soon will I be able to return?

If you don't feel comfortable dropping in—because of your appearance or because you're not prepared—then you probably should return to apply for the job later.

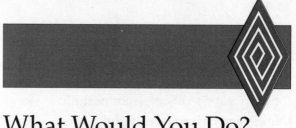

What Would You Do?

You have gone for a summer walk in shorts and sandals. On the way, you pass a restaurant with a "help wanted" sign. You have been looking for a job in a restaurant, and this place looks like it might attract the sort of customers who tip well. You're afraid that if you miss this opportunity, someone else will get the job. You're also concerned that your appearance might turn off a potential employer. What would you do?

Understanding Help-Wanted Ads

Another place to look for jobs is in the classified ad sections of local newspapers. Many employers place advertisements in the classifieds when they need to fill jobs.

There are new job ads in most newspapers every day. The Sunday newspapers usually carry the greatest number of job ads. Often the classified ads are published in a pull-out section of the paper.

Small newspapers sometimes devote the last few pages to the classified section. Larger newspapers have an index on the front page that tells you what's in each section of the newspaper. Those sections may be identified by letters—section A, section B, and so on—and then by page numbers. If the front

ABBREVIATIONS USED IN HELP-WANTED ADS

The following chart can help you translate common abbreviations used in help-wanted classified ads.

Abbreviation	Meaning	Abbreviation	Meaning
avail.	available	mo.	month
exp.	experience	pref.	prefer, preferred
FT, ft	full-time	PT, pt	part-time
hr.	hour	ref.	references
HS, hs	high school	req.	require, required
immed.	immediate	sal.	salary
K (as in $10K)	thousand	sec'y	secretary
M (as in $10M)	million	tel.	telephone
max.	maximum	w/	with
min.	minimum	wk.	week, work
M-F	Monday through Friday	wpm, w.p.m.	words per minute

page index of a paper says the classified ads begin on B-3, you would turn to page 3 of section B.

Job listings generally appear in the help-wanted category. Within that category, job listings are usually in alphabetical order by job title. Job titles may vary from one newspaper to another, so it's a good idea to scan the entire help-wanted category in the index.

Blind Ads

Some help-wanted ads do not include the employer's name, address, or telephone number. These are called **blind ads** because you don't know whom you are responding to. To reply to a blind ad, you must send a letter to a box number at the newspaper's address. This address may be listed on the front page of the employment classified section. If you can't find it, call the newspaper and ask for the employment classified address.

Employers may place blind ads because they don't want to receive phone calls, or because they don't want their employees to know they're advertising. If you answer a blind ad, don't be surprised if you don't get a reply. Employers who place these ads usually do not respond to all applicants.

Replying to Help-Wanted Ads

Keep the following points in mind if you use the classified section of the newspaper when starting your job search.

♦ **Read the job ads early each day.** Respond immediately to any ad that interests you. If you wait too long, the job may get filled.

♦ **Look for the qualifications.** Ads usually list the qualifications for jobs. Some employers list several qualifications. If you have some of the qualifications listed in the ad, then apply for the job. While employers may look for an ideal candidate, they often accept one who has many, but not all of the qualifications.

♦ **Inquire by phone.** If a job ad lists a telephone number but no address, call the number and ask how to apply for the job. Most employers want to see an application, and they want to see you in person.

♦ **Apply in person.** When an ad provides an address and says "Apply in person," go to that address and be prepared to meet with the employer. Make sure you are dressed appropriately. If the ad specifies a time to show up, be sure to get there on time. Employers look for employees who are punctual, and it's important to make a good first impression.

♦ **Write to the employer.** Some ads list an address and tell applicants to write. In that case, you must send the employer a letter to ask for a job interview. (You will read more about application letters in Section 3.)

♦ **Read the ads carefully.** Avoid ads for jobs that say you must invest money or purchase sample merchandise. Also beware of any job ad that says applicants must pay for their own training. Be careful of ads that make big promises about how much you can earn.

♦ **Keep a list of the ads you answer.** Keep a notebook in which you record the ads that you respond to. That way you can refer to your list when an employer contacts you.

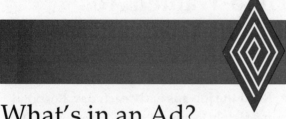

What's in an Ad?

Read the help-wanted ad below. On the lines following the ad, write out the words that are abbreviated in the ad. Then answer the questions that follow.

> **WORD PROCESSOR** Major corp. in downtown Chgo. has immed. FT opening for exp'd. word processor. Position will provide w.p. and gen'l clerical support for various depts. incl. relief for receptionist. Must have w.p. and gen'l clerical skills. Min. 3 yrs. w.p. exp. and type 55 wpm. Competitive sal. and exc. benefit pkg. offered. Write to Bob Clark, P.O. Box 98911, Chicago, IL 60680.

_____

_____

_____

_____

_____

1. What job is being advertised?

_____

2. What are the qualifications?

_____

3. Is a salary listed?

_____

4. Where is the job located?

_____

5. How should applicants respond?

_____

6. Whom should they respond to?

_____

Resources to Help in the Job Hunt

Another way to find a job is to call or write to companies that you want to work for. Your telephone book will help you do that.

In the front of your local telephone book, you can find helpful information about using the book and the telephone itself. Most telephone books include white pages and yellow pages.

The white pages list the names of individuals, businesses, and other organizations in alphabetical order, with their telephone numbers. The listings may include street addresses, too.

The yellow pages are an alphabetical listing of companies, stores, and professional firms along with their telephone numbers and addresses. The yellow pages are divided into business categories, such as "Boat Yards" and "Messenger Services."

When you call a company, ask for the **personnel department** or the human resources department, the company department that is in charge of hiring. Personnel workers will be able to tell you if the company has job openings or apprenticeship programs. **Apprentices** earn wages as they learn a trade by working in it for a certain amount of time. If there are openings, ask the personnel worker when you can visit the company to fill out an application form. For smaller companies that have no personnel department, you may need to talk to a department supervisor or foreman who has the power to hire.

You can also use telephone books to find the phone numbers and addresses of **labor unions**. These are organizations that bargain with employers on behalf of workers. Labor unions may know about job openings in specific fields, or they may be sponsoring specific apprenticeships.

You can also find listings of employers' names and telephone numbers in other directories published by business associations. For example, the Chamber of Commerce in your community may publish a directory of its members. You can find copies of industrial and service directories for your state and nearby states at your local library. These directories usually list company information in three ways: alphabetically, geographically, and by product. Company listings provide such information as:

♦ **company name, address, and telephone number**
♦ **number of employees**
♦ **the type of product or service offered**
♦ **sales volume or range**
♦ **year the company was established**
♦ **names of principal officers**

The federal government publishes two directories about apprenticeships. One is *The National Apprenticeship Program and Apprenticeship Information*, and the other is *A Woman's Guide to Apprenticeship*. If the library doesn't have these directories, you can get copies by writing to the U.S. Department of Labor, 200 Constitution Avenue NW, Washington, D.C. 20210.

Hidden Jobs

Many other job leads can be found in newspapers. These job leads are "hidden" because they're not specific advertisements in help-wanted sections. Instead they're leads you get by reading about businesses. Smaller community papers and the business section of larger papers are good sources of the following kinds of information:

♦ **New businesses and industries.** New businesses opening in an area often need to hire many new employees.
♦ **Transfers and promotions.** When an employee receives a transfer or promotion, the employer may have a new job opening. A **promotion** is an advance in position or rank within a company.

Practice Using the Yellow Pages

The column on page 18 is from a yellow pages directory. Use this information to locate the listings for the following business categories:

1. Marketing Consultants   Pages _____
2. Media Brokers   Pages _____
3. Mechanical Engineers   Pages _____
4. Meat Packers   Pages _____
5. Mason Contractors   Pages _____

What's in a Company Entry?

The entry below is from a state industrial directory. Read it, and answer the questions.

POWELL CHEMICAL CORP.
83 Walnut Street
Powell, NY 10025
Phone: 315-555-9876
Products: Plastics,
Fragrances, Agricultural
Chemicals
Sales: $22M
Emp: 1,500
Pres—D. Jeffrey Walters
SrVP—Helen Miller
SrVP—Fin—Ron Stoudt

1. What does this company manufacture?

_____

2. How many people work there?

_____

3. What is the company's address?

_____

4. What is the company's annual sales volume?

_____

5. How many company officers are listed?

_____

Contacting State Employment Services

You might want to check your state employment office for a list of job openings in your area. This office may also have information about apprenticeship programs.

You don't have to pay for the services offered by a state employment office. This office can help all job hunters, especially people who have trouble finding work, such as people who did not finish high school or those who speak little or no English.

You can find the location and phone number of your state employment office by looking in your telephone book under the name of your state. Some state employment offices may be called the "Job Service." If your telephone book has blue pages that list government offices, you will find the number there. Otherwise, look in the white pages under your state's name, then "Labor Department," then "Employment Services."

If you visit the state employment office, you will fill out a form requiring information about your work history and your skills. Take with you as much information as you can about your educational background and work history. A counselor will read the form and then talk with you to work out a plan so that you can find a job.

Help with Special Problems

Many national organizations sponsor programs that offer counseling, training, and other support services for people who face special problems in finding jobs. You can go to these organizations to find out what help is available in your community. Here are some of the groups for whom such help is available:

♦ **The visually impaired:**
Job Opportunities for the Blind
1-800-638-7518.

♦ **The handicapped:**
The President's Committee on Employment of the Handicapped
1111 20th St. NW, Room 636
Washington, D.C. 20036

(continued)

♦ **Minorities:**
League of United Latin American Citizens National Educational Service Centers Inc.
400 First St. NW, Suite 716
Washington, D.C. 20001
National Association for the Advancement of Colored People (NAACP)
4805 Mount Hope Dr.
Baltimore, MD 21215-3297

♦ **Older workers:**
National Association of Older Workers Employment Services
c/o National Council on Aging
600 Maryland Ave. SW
Washington, D.C. 20024

♦ **Women:**
United States Department of Labor Women's Bureau
200 Constitution Ave. NW
Washington, D.C. 20210
Catalyst
250 Park Ave. South
New York, NY 10003
Wider Opportunities for Women
1325 G St. NW
Lower Level
Washington, D.C. 20005

Many of these organizations have offices in major cities throughout the country.

Telephone Tips

The impression you make over the telephone can help you get a job. Keep these points in mind when you call about job openings:

♦ **Call from a quiet, private place.** You don't want to be interrupted.

- **Speak clearly.** Be sure the other person can hear you. Don't talk too fast. Pronounce words carefully.
- **Ask for the correct person.** For a small business, ask to speak to the manager. For a large company, ask for the personnel department.
- **Identify yourself.** State your first and last name and the reason for your call before you ask any questions.
- **Be courteous.** Speak in a friendly tone of voice. Thank anyone who helps you.
- **Mention contacts right away.** If you have permission to use someone's name, mention the name as soon as you identify yourself. Also mention what the person told you. For example, an applicant might say, "This is Joe Stevens. Jerry Greenburg suggested that I call you. He said you might have an opening in your shipping department."
- **Ask if the employer wants to meet with you.** If you schedule an appointment, write down the time and date. Repeat it to the person who gave you the information to be sure it is correct.
- **Ask important questions.** Before you decide if you're interested in a job, you should ask about certain details. They include the hours, specific duties, and the exact location of the job.
- **Get people's names.** Write down the names of people you speak to, in case you need to contact them again. Before you hang up, be sure you can spell and pronounce their names correctly.

Exploring Civil Service Opportunities

The government is another source of jobs. More people work for the government than for any other business organization in the United States. Governments at all levels—federal, state, and local—need workers to carry out the tasks of government. These workers include road repairers, mail carriers, and office workers. Most people who hold federal, state, or local government jobs are **civil service workers.**

Civil service jobs require applicants to take competitive examinations. There are books that can help you prepare for civil service examinations. These books are available in many public libraries and may be purchased at larger bookstores.

You can find the locations and phone numbers of the civil service offices in your community in your telephone book. For the federal civil service office, look under "United States Government Office of Personnel Management" or "Merit Systems Protection Board." For state and local civil service offices, call the general information numbers for your state, county, or local government to find out how to apply for civil service jobs.

To practice finding information in the telephone book, use it to locate the names of the federal, state, and city or county civil service offices nearest you. Write their addresses and telephone numbers in the blank spaces that follow.

Federal Office of Personnel Management

Address: _____

Phone: _____

State civil service office

Address: _____

Phone: _____

City/County civil service office

Address: _____

Phone: _____

OTHER OPTIONS FOR JOB HUNTING

Option	What It Is	Where to Turn
Advertisements	Situation-wanted ads can be placed in newspapers or in fliers that you distribute yourself. This is especially useful if you are experienced, have recently moved into a new area, or are providing a service such as babysitting.	Ads should be placed in local newspapers or trade or professional journals. Fliers should be placed on bulletin boards or distributed to homes or businesses.
Career Placement Offices	These offices list employers' job openings, provide job counseling, and help people plan their job search. Only students and recent graduates can use the services of Career Placement Offices.	Career placement offices are located at trade and technical schools, community colleges, colleges, and universities.
Company Personnel Offices	Most larger companies have a human resources or personnel department. If you want a job in a specific company, you can call or go to this office to apply.	Look for companies in the yellow pages of the phone book or in industrial or service directories.
Employment Agencies	Private agencies may specialize in finding jobs for people in certain fields, or they may handle all types of jobs. Be sure to check the agency's reputation and the fees you have to pay for their services.	Employment agencies may put ads in the help-wanted section of the classifieds in newspapers. You can also look in the yellow pages of phone books under "Employment Agencies."
Job Clubs	These support groups are usually run by nonprofit organizations. They may provide counseling, career development, and job placement services.	Churches, community organizations, schools, synagogues, and youth groups often have job clubs.
Job Fairs	These "fairs" may be sponsored by schools, businesses, or trade or professional organizations. A large number of employers are available at booths to talk to job hunters about opportunities.	Job fairs may be advertised in local newspapers, at career placement offices, and on bulletin boards.
Temporary Job Agencies	These are private employment agencies that hire people to work at temporary jobs. Temporary jobs are a good way to gain work experience and make personal contacts. Jobs may lead to offers of full-time work.	Temporary job agencies may put ads in the help-wanted section of the classifieds in newspapers. You can also look in the yellow pages of phone books under "Employment Contractors—Temporary Help."

The chart shows seven additional places to look for jobs. If you want to know more about any of them, ask your program coordinator.

Points to Remember

In this section, you learned that there are many ways to find jobs. Some of the most important include:
♦ networking with friends, relatives, and acquaintances
♦ reading and responding to help-wanted signs
♦ reading and replying to help-wanted ads
♦ using directories and guides to find possible employers
♦ contacting your state employment offices
♦ exploring civil service jobs in your area

✓ CHECKPOINT ✓

Word-Wise

Fill in the blanks below to explain some important points about looking for a job. The answers are key terms introduced in this section.

There are many good ways to look for a job. One way is by _____ with friends and relatives. Another way is to look in the help-wanted ads. Employers sometimes place _____ _____ in which the company name, address, and telephone number are not given. You can also call a company to find out about job openings. You should ask for the _____ _____ , which is in charge of hiring. If you drop in on an employer, you might have an _____, during which you will answer questions and fill out an application form.

Putting It to Work

Your 18-year-old brother is looking for a job as a store clerk. He has been looking in the help-wanted ads but hasn't found anything that interests him. He has come to you for advice on how to look for a job. What will you tell him?

_____

_____

_____

You Be the Judge

You are looking for a job by networking with friends and relatives. A friend told you about a job opening at the company where she works. The opening was posted on the employee bulletin board. Your friend's company advertises job openings for their own employees before placing ads for the general public in newspapers. You might get your friend in trouble if you answer the ad now, but it sounds like just the type of work you were looking for. What would you do?

_____

_____

_____

_____

Getting the Facts

Talk to five friends, relatives, or acquaintances about how they found their current jobs. List each person's first name and the method by which he or she heard about the job.

1. _____
2. _____
3. _____
4. _____
5. _____

SECTION 3

TAKING THE NEXT STEPS

Steve walked into the warehouse office. A woman was typing at a desk. "May I help you?" she asked.

"Yes. I want to apply for the stock clerk job. My name's Steve Taylor," he said.

"Just a minute," she replied.

She picked up the phone. Steve watched the forklifts in the warehouse while she talked on the phone.

After she hung up, she said, "Mr. D'Angelo will be with you soon. Please fill this out while you wait." She held out a pen and an application form.

"You can have a seat over there," she said as she pointed to a chair.

Steve took the form and the pen and sat down. He carefully read both sides of the application. Then he pulled notes from his pocket. Referring to them, he filled out his social security number, the names and addresses of schools he had attended, and the addresses and dates of places he had worked. Then he checked over the form.

He stood up and held out the form. "I'm finished. Should I give this to you?"

"No," she replied. "You can give it to Mr. D'Angelo when he gets here."

"OK," Steve said.

"Here he comes now," the receptionist said.

Steve turned just in time to see a large man in shirtsleeves enter the office. "Hi, Janet," he said.

Then he walked over to Steve and shook his hand. "Hi, I'm Vince D'Angelo, the manager here. I understand you're interested in the stock clerk job."

"Yes, Mr. D'Angelo, I am. I saw the sign in your window."

"Good," Mr. D'Angelo said with a smile. "Follow me to my office and we'll take a look at your application."

Applying for Jobs in Person

When Steve walked into the warehouse office, he didn't have an appointment. He had seen a help-wanted sign in the window. And he had decided to apply for the job.

Many people apply for jobs this way. Some of them see a help-wanted sign on a bulletin board or in a store window. Others may see a help-wanted ad that asks applicants to apply in person.

There are several advantages to looking for a job this way. You get the chance to observe workers and to check out the working environment. You get to fill out application forms. You also get experience in meeting with employers, talking about jobs, and describing your assets. Each time you do this, it becomes easier, and you gain more confidence.

Applying in person can be one of the most effective ways of getting a job, if you know how to go about it. You learned how to decide whether you were prepared enough to drop in on an employer in Section 2. Now let's look at what to do when you actually drop in.

♦ Don't drop in unless you are dressed appropriately for an interview.

♦ When you introduce yourself, say what the purpose of your visit is right away. Smile and look the other person in the eye. Shake hands firmly, if it's appropriate.

♦ If the time isn't convenient for the employer, try to set up an appointment.

♦ Be enthusiastic, polite, and confident. You want to show that you're interested in the job and that you feel you're capable of doing the work.

♦ Be prepared to fill out an application form. See the feature on this page for information on how to prepare ahead of time.

♦ If you're interviewed, participate in the interview by asking questions. Learn as much as you can about the job and the company. Asking questions shows that you're interested.

♦ Before you leave, thank the interviewer or the person who took your application. Ask when a decision will be made about the job.

♦ Send the interviewer a thank-you note.

Preparing to Complete Application Forms

Steve Taylor carried a page of notes in his pocket when he applied for the job at the warehouse. He knew that the notes would help him fill in all the details on an application form.

You can be prepared, too, by making your own notes of the following:

♦ **Your Social Security number.**

♦ **Your visa number—passport approval—and the expiration date.** This is necessary only if you are not a citizen of the United States.

♦ **The names and addresses of schools you attended and special courses you took.** Also include the dates when you attended them.

♦ **The names, addresses, and telephone numbers of your last three employers.** Also include your supervisors' names and the dates when you started and left.

♦ **The pay for your last three jobs.** Include how much you were earning when you started and when you left.

♦ **The names, addresses, and telephone numbers of three people who would recommend you for a job.** These **references** can include past employers or people who know your skills and abilities, such as teachers or coaches. Before you list people as references, get their permission and confirm what they will say about you. Also, make sure their phone numbers and addresses are up-to-date.

Who Can You Ask to Be Your References?

In the blank spaces that follow, write the names of three people you could ask to be references for you. Then explain why each person would be a good reference to have.

Name	Why Person Would Be a Good Reference
Example: Carol Hall	Supervisor at previous job; was very happy with my work.

1. _____ _____

2. _____ _____

3. _____ _____

Filling Out Job Application Forms

The first time you visit an employer, you will probably be given an application form to complete. The form may be one or two pages. It may be a photocopy or it may be printed. Application forms may look different, but they all serve the same purpose. They provide a convenient way for employers to get information about applicants' backgrounds and qualifications.

Employers often use these forms to make hiring decisions, so fill them out neatly, accurately, and completely. Keep the following points in mind when you fill out an application form:

♦ **Before you begin writing, look over the whole form carefully.** Read the instructions, and notice where different information goes.

This will help you avoid mistakes that can make the form look messy. If you don't understand the instructions, ask questions. Follow the directions that the instructions give.

♦ **Use a pen with black or dark blue ink.** Don't use a pencil. Unless directed otherwise, print your answers, and write slowly and carefully. If the employer can't read your writing, your application may be thrown away.

♦ **Write your proper name on the application form.** Don't write your nickname.

♦ **Answer all of the questions on the form.** If a question doesn't apply to you, write the letters *NA* (for "not applicable") in that space. This shows that you haven't missed any questions. You may also use *NA* if there are certain personal questions on the form that may invade your privacy. Those questions concern age, marital status, race, religion, sex, nationality, or physical or mental handicaps.

♦ **Answer all questions truthfully.** Employers usually call references, past employers, and schools to confirm the information on application forms. If the employer finds out that you provided false information, you won't get the job.

♦ **If you were found guilty of a felony, answer truthfully.** Employers often include a question about **felony** convictions on applications. If you were involved in a serious crime, be prepared to tell an interviewer about it.

♦ **Read over the completed application form before you turn it in.** Be sure that you have answered all the questions. Check for misspellings and other errors. If you need to make corrections, make them as neatly as possible.

♦ **Sign the application form.** Do this only after you have read all the fine print. When you sign a form, you are certifying that the information you have written is accurate. You may also be agreeing to certain conditions, or procedures, such as drug testing.

Practice Filling Out Application Forms

Pick a job that interests you. Imagine that you are applying for that job.

Fill out the job application form on page 27 with information about the job you have made up. Complete it with real information about your background. When you apply for real jobs, you can use the background information on this form as your notes.

Writing Application Letters

Some employers want applicants to send **application letters** before applying in person. Employers who require these letters usually ask for them specifically.

Employers may do this so that they can review applicants' qualifications before taking the time to meet with them. Sometimes employers ask for letters because they know that an applicant who takes the time to write a letter is really interested in the job. Other employers may want a letter as a sample of each applicant's writing skills.

The purpose of an application letter is to persuade employers to interview you and consider you for jobs. You can help to accomplish this by following these guidelines:

♦ **Use standard English.** Don't use slang. If you're not sure of how to spell a word, look it up in a dictionary.

♦ **Send the letter to a specific person, if possible.** Some help-wanted ads give the name of the person to whom you should write. If you don't have a specific name, you can call

and ask to whom to send the letter. If you can't get a specific person's name, address your letter to the personnel department. If it's a blind ad, follow the directions in the ad.

♦ **Use a formal greeting with the person's last name and title, if possible.** This line introduces the letter. If you are writing to Jonas Robinson, the greeting should say, "Dear Mr. Robinson:" If you don't know the person's name, write "Dear Sir or Madam:"

♦ **Start the body of the letter by telling the employer why you are writing.** Say which job you're interested in and why.

♦ **Then tell the employer why you're qualified for the job.** Include highlights of your work experience, education, and other qualifications. Describe any special skills you have. Don't mention any qualifications you lack.

♦ **In the last paragraph, ask the employer for a chance to meet with him or her.** Don't forget to say when and where you can be reached.

♦ **Check your letter carefully before you mail it.** If possible, ask someone else to read it. Another person may see errors that you missed. Employers sometimes reject applicants if they find errors in their letters.

Business Letter Writing Tips

The way an application letter looks is almost as important as what it says. If you follow the guidelines on page 28 when you write an application letter, you will make a good impression on employers.

After reading the tips on writing a business letter, you will find tips on addressing a business envelope. The neatness and accuracy of the envelope is extremely important. After addressing the envelope, folding the letter, and enclosing it, be sure to seal the envelope and put the correct amount of postage on it.

APPLICATION FOR EMPLOYMENT

NAME (LAST)	(FIRST)	(MIDDLE)	SOCIAL SECURITY NO.

PRESENT ADDRESS	CITY	STATE	ZIP CODE	AREA CODE	TELEPHONE NO.

PERMANENT ADDRESS (IF DIFFERENT FROM ABOVE)	AREA CODE	TELEPHONE NO.

POSITION APPLIED FOR	DATE AVAILABLE

SALARY OR WAGE DESIRED	WILL YOU RELOCATE?	REFERRED BY

ARE YOU A U. S. CITIZEN? ☐ YES ☐ NO	IF NOT A U. S. CITIZEN, LIST VISA NUMBER AND EXPIRATION DATE NUMBER _____ DATE _____

WITHIN THE LAST 5 YEARS HAVE YOU BEEN CONVICTED OF A FELONY?	☐ NO ☐ YES	IF YES, GIVE DETAILS ON BACK PAGE	HAVE YOU EVER BEEN EMPLOYED BY OUR COMPANY? IF YES, GIVE DETAILS ON BACK PAGE

EDUCATION	INSTITUTION NAME AND ADDRESS	DID YOU GRADUATE?	MAJOR FIELD OF STUDY	CLASS STANDING
HIGH				
SCHOOL				
COLLEGE OR				
UNIVERSITY				
GRADUATE				
STUDY				
OTHER				

EMPLOYMENT RECORD	PLEASE LIST PAST THREE EMPLOYERS, STARTING WITH MOST RECENT. INCLUDE U. S. ARMED FORCES AND VOLUNTARY SERVICES.

LIST YOUR MOST RECENT POSITION HELD	MAY WE CONTACT YOUR PRESENT EMPLOYER? ☐ YES ☐ NO

EMPLOYER'S NAME AND COMPLETE ADDRESS/PHONE	DATES EMPLOYED		POSITION TITLE
	FROM	TO	NAME AND TITLE OF SUPERVISOR
	SALARY		
	START	FINAL	REASON FOR LEAVING

EMPLOYER'S NAME AND COMPLETE ADDRESS/PHONE	DATES EMPLOYED		POSITION TITLE
	FROM	TO	NAME AND TITLE OF SUPERVISOR
	SALARY		
	START	FINAL	REASON FOR LEAVING

EMPLOYER'S NAME AND COMPLETE ADDRESS/PHONE	DATES EMPLOYED		POSITION TITLE
	FROM	TO	NAME AND TITLE OF SUPERVISOR
	SALARY		
	START	FINAL	REASON FOR LEAVING

GUIDELINES FOR WRITING APPLICATION LETTERS

Use plain white, 8 1/2-by-11-inch bond paper and write on only one side. Type the letter single spaced.

Leave a 1-inch margin on the right and left and at the top and bottom of each page.

① 882 Hickory Road
Highland, CA 90144
October 19, 199X ②

③ Mr. Ron Owens
Ron's Service Station
21 Greentree Avenue
Highland, CA 90123
④
Dear Mr. Owens:
⑤
Please consider my application for the auto mechanic's position you advertised in The News on October 17.

⑥ I am a recent graduate of Cole County Vocational-Technical School, where I studied to be an auto mechanic. I have worked part-time for the past two years as a gas station attendant. In my spare time I help my uncle restore old cars. My schedule is flexible and would allow me to work days, evenings, or weekends.

⑥ I would appreciate an interview with you to talk about my qualifications for the job. You may reach me at (213) 555-6256.

⑦ Sincerely,

Joseph J. Russo   ⑨

⑧ Joseph J. Russo

① Type your address in the upper right or left corner. Use one line for your street address and the next line for your city, state, and zip code.

② Type the date under the address.

③ Leave two blank lines after the date. Then, at the left margin, type the employer's name and business address. Use one line for the person's name (or personnel department), the next line for the name of the company, the next line for the street address, and the next line for the city, state, and zip code.

④ Skip a line after the employer's address.

⑤ Then, at the left margin, type the greeting. Skip a line after the greeting. Put a colon (:) after the greeting.

⑥ Within the body of the letter, skip a line after each paragraph.

⑦ After the body of the letter, skip a line and type the closing. This is the word or phrase that ends the letter. Closings to use in a business letter include "Sincerely," "Sincerely yours," and "Truly yours." The closing should line up with your address and the date. It should be followed by a comma.

⑧ Skip four lines after the closing, then type your name so that it lines up with the closing.

⑨ In the space between the closing and your typed name, neatly sign your name.

Joseph J. Russo
882 Hickory Road
Highland, CA 90144

③ Mr. Ron Owens
Ron's Service Station
21 Greentree Avenue
Highland, CA 90123

① Use a standard white business envelope, 4 inches by 9 1/2 inches.

② Type your name and address in the upper left

corner of the envelope.

③ Type the employer's name and address in the center of the envelope.

Practice Writing an Application Letter

In a newspaper, find a help-wanted ad that you're interested in answering. On a separate piece of paper, write a letter of application. Use the sample on page 28 as a guide. Then answer these questions.

1. Have I used an appropriate greeting?

_____

2. Have I explained why I am writing?

_____

3. Does the letter indicate what kind of job I am seeking?

_____

4. Have I stated my most important qualifications for this job?

_____

5. Have I said anything negative?

_____

6. Have I asked for an interview?

_____

7. Is the letter likely to make the employer interested in me?

_____

8. Have I signed the letter?

_____

Writing Cover Letters

A **cover letter** is set up like an application letter, but its purpose is different. A cover letter's main purpose is to get an employer to read the attached resume. A **resume** is a written summary of your background and qualifications. Resumes will be discussed later in this section.

The guidelines below will show you how to write a cover letter like the one on page 30:

♦ Start the body of a cover letter by stating why you are writing it. If you're sending a

A SAMPLE COVER LETTER

```
1010 Payne Drive
Smith Village, NY 10344
June 5, 199X



Mr. Michael Williams
Personnel Director
Park Insurance Company
One Park Plaza
Oakwood, NY 10457

Dear Mr. Williams:

I would like to apply for the position of secretary
that you advertised in today's Oakwood Times.

As you can see from the enclosed resume, I have both
educational training and clerical work experience. My
typing speed is 65 words per minute. My steno speed
is 100 words per minute. I am very eager to advance
into a secretarial position such as the one you have
available. I feel that, given a chance, I will be an
asset to your company.

I would like to meet with you to discuss my
qualifications for this job. You can contact me at
914-555-1865. If there is no answer at this number,
you may call 914-555-9087 and leave a message.

Sincerely,

Lara Roberts

Lara Roberts
```

A cover letter is different from an application letter in one main way—it refers to your resume.

resume because you heard about a job opening, say where you heard about the job. If someone the employer knows has suggested that you write, mention that person's name if he or she gave you permission to do so.

♦ In a sentence or two, explain why you think you're the right person for the job.

♦ Always refer to your resume in a cover letter. You might want to do this by calling the employer's attention to a particular fact in your resume.

♦ In the last paragraph, ask the employer to contact you. You might say, "I would like to meet with you to discuss my qualifications," or, "You can reach me at (215) 555-5982."

Practice Writing a Cover Letter

You are sending your resume to the Alpha Company. Your friend Joelle Dunbar is a supervisor there. She told you that the company is hiring now and is looking for people with your qualifications.

She suggested that you send your resume to Harold Freeman and gave you permission to mention her name.

On a separate sheet of paper, write a cover letter for your resume. Use the sample cover letter on page 30 as a guide. After you write the letter, check off the items listed below:

♦ Have I explained why I am writing?

♦ Does the letter indicate what kind of job I am seeking?

♦ Have I stated why I think I am the right person for this job?

♦ Have I referred to my resume?

♦ Have I asked the employer to contact me?

♦ Does this letter call attention to my resume in a favorable way?

Preparing a Resume

There may be times during your job search when you have to provide an employer with a resume. Not all jobs require resumes, though nowadays many employers are asking to see them. You probably won't need one to find a job in mechanical trades, such as auto repair, manufacturing, or construction. In general, you don't need to provide a resume unless an employer asks for one.

A resume serves the same purpose as an application letter. It is used to persuade an employer to consider you for a job.

Your resume should tell the employer what kind of job you want, what kind of work you have done so far, and what schools you have attended. It may also include additional information, such as awards you've received or interests you may have outside of work. Resumes should be brief. But they should contain more detailed information than letters of application.

You can target a resume to a specific job with one employer. Or you can target it to several employers. If you are sending it to one employer, you should highlight the information that relates to that particular job. A resume that you send to several employers should be more general.

Whether you prepare a general resume or a resume for a specific job, there are certain guidelines to follow. As you read the items that follow, refer to the sample resume on page 32.

♦ **Name, address, and telephone number.** If necessary, you may include both your temporary and your permanent addresses and phone numbers here. However, most people only list their current phone number and address. It is a good idea to provide a number where you can receive a message if you can't be reached.

♦ **Objective.** This statement should describe the kind of work you are seeking now. If you

SETTING UP YOUR RESUME

Type your resume or have someone type it for you. Use plain white, 8 1/2-by-11-inch paper. Try to limit the information on your resume to a single page. If necessary, you can use two pages. Type on one side of the paper only.

Leave a 1-inch margin on the right and left and at the top and bottom of each page.

Pay attention to the resume's appearance. Use spacing and underlining to make certain items stand out. That way, the employer can see the most important information right away.

① Type your name, address, and telephone number at the top. This information can go either on the left or in the center.

② Skip a line. Then type your objective.

③ Skip a line. Then type your first heading (Work Experience or Education).

④ Skip a line between each job or school under the heading.

⑤ Skip a line. Then type your second heading (Work Experience or Education).

⑥ Skip a line between each item under the heading.

```
                              ①
                        Lara Roberts
                        1010 Payne Drive
                        Smith Village, NY 10344
                        Telephone: 914-555-1865

②  Objective:        Position as Secretary
③  Work Experience
   June 1989         Receptionist/Typist, The Smith Village News.
        to           Answer phones, do typing and filing. Do some
   Present           data entry on computer.
④
   Sept. 1986        Office Assistant, part time.
        to           Dr. Jane Ortiz, Smith Village.
   April 1989        Answered phones, did typing and filing, helped
                     process insurance claims.

⑤  Education         Smith County Community College, Certificate in
                     Business and Office Skills. One-year program
                     completed May 1990.

                     Courses included Information Systems, Word
                     Processing, Communications, and Business Math.
        ⑥
                     Hamilton High School, Smith Village.
                     Graduated June 1989, average B+.
                     Courses included typing, steno, bookkeeping,
        ⑦            and introduction to the personal computer. Was
                     recipient of Mary S. Hamilton Business Award
                     given to outstanding student taking commercial
                     courses.
```

⑦ You don't have to write complete sentences. Omitting the "I" or "my" from statements will help you keep your resume short. For example, instead of saying, "My duties included typing correspondence, filing, and answering telephones," you can say, "Duties included..." or "Typed correspondence, filed..."

Use action words, such as managed, directed, led, and supervised.

Check your resume carefully before you send it out. Ask someone else to read it. Another person might find mistakes that you missed. If you need to send copies of your resume to several employers, get photocopies made. You can have this done at any copying store.

will be sending your resume to several employers, be sure to write a general objective so that it will apply to all of the jobs.

♦ **Work experience.** Start this section with a heading such as "Work Experience" or "Experience." Begin the listing with your current or most recent job. If you have lots of experience, limit your list to the most recent or most important jobs. As a rule, you need only go back 10 years.

For each job, state the employer's name and location, the months and years when you started and left the job, and the position or positions you held. Include a brief description of your responsibilities in each position. The description should show which skills you used in the job. For example, if you worked as a receptionist, you might list, "Answered telephone, directed calls, greeted visitors, sorted mail."

If you have little or no paid work experience, list your role as a homemaker, part-time and summer jobs, as well as volunteer work you have done. Just be sure to identify them accordingly.

Start your job listings with the information you want to stress. You can start with either your title or the company name, for example. No matter which you choose, use the same format for each job.

♦ **Education.** Start this section with a heading, such as "Education" or "Education and Training." List the schools you have attended and the diplomas, degrees, or certificates you have received. Employers want to know the highest level of education you have attained, so start with the most recent school and work backwards.

List each school on a separate line. Include the school's name and location, the years you attended the school, and the diploma, degree, or certificate you earned.

If you took courses or participated in school clubs or other activities that provided you with particular skills, list them. If you

earned high grades, scholarships, or other academic distinctions, be sure to mention them. (If you don't have much work experience, you may want to organize your resume so that the education heading and information comes before the work heading and information.)

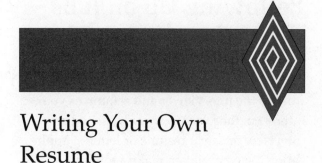

Writing Your Own Resume

It's a good idea to have a resume on hand when you're looking for a job. You never know when an employer will ask you for one.

The first step in writing a resume is deciding what information to include. The questions below can help you decide what to put on your resume.

1. What personal information should I list at the top of my resume?

_____

_____

2. What is my objective?

_____

_____

3. Which jobs should I list?

_____

_____

_____

4. Which education and training do I want to highlight?

_____

_____

On a separate sheet of paper, construct a rough draft of your resume. Use the information under "Preparing a Resume" and on your application form on page 27 to help you construct the resume. The example on page 32 can help you organize your information.

Following Up on Jobs

After you have had an interview with an employer, send a thank-you note immediately. The thank-you note keeps your name in front of the interviewer and reinforces your interest in the job. After you have had an interview or sent a resume or letter of application to an employer, make a follow-up call within two weeks. Don't wait for employers to call you.

The follow-up call serves several purposes:

♦ It shows that you're still interested in the job. And it shows that you're willing to make an extra effort.

♦ It demonstrates your ability to follow through—an asset that many employers want in an employee.

♦ It may help you stand out from dozens of other applicants who didn't make follow-up calls.

♦ If you aren't offered the job, the person you call could refer you to another department or company.

When you make a follow-up call, say that you're still interested in the job. Try to find out when the employer expects to make a hiring decision.

Making follow-up calls will be easier if you keep careful records of your job search. Keep a notebook with a page for each employer you contact. Make notes about each application letter or resume you send, each application form you fill out, and each conversation you have with an employer. Write down the date, purpose, and outcome of each contact and the name of the person you dealt with.

Following Up

Suppose you are calling an employer on the telephone to follow up on a letter of application that you sent a week ago. You sent the letter in response to an ad in the newspaper. First decide the type of company and the job that's available.

Role-play the situation with another student. One person takes the role of the job hunter. The other takes the role of the employer. After you play one role, switch and try the other. Then answer the following questions.

1. How did you feel in the role of the job hunter?

_____

_____

2. What do you feel you did well?

_____

_____

3. What do you need to improve?

_____

_____

4. How could you make that improvement?

_____

_____

Points to Remember

In this section, you learned the many ways of making contact with employers. Some of the most important include:

♦ applying for jobs in person

♦ filling out job application forms

♦ writing and sending application letters

♦ writing and sending resumes

♦ following up on interviews with a thank-you note and a call

CHECKPOINT

Word-Wise

Fill in the blanks below to complete the sentences. The answers are key terms introduced in this section.

1. _____ are people who can tell an employer about your work, your skills, or your talents.

2. An employer may ask if you have ever been convicted of a _____ , which is a serious crime.

3. A summary of your job qualifications is called a _____.

4. When you send a resume, you should send a _____ _____ with it.

Putting It to Work

You have seen a help-wanted sign in a store window. You decide to return later to apply in person for the job. Make a list of four things you should write down so you will be prepared when you apply for the job.

1. _____
2. _____
3. _____
4. _____

You Be the Judge

You have decided to apply for a job in person. The receptionist handed you an application form to fill out. After a few minutes, the interviewer came out to greet you, but you had not had time to finish filling out the application form. What would you do?

_____
_____
_____
_____
_____
_____
_____
_____

Getting the Facts

Look at the cover letter and sample resume on pages 30 and 32 to answer the following questions.

1. To whom is the letter addressed?

_____

2. What job is the applicant interested in?

_____

3. Why does the applicant feel that she is the right person for the job?

_____
_____

4. What is the objective listed on the resume?

_____

5. What is the most recent work experience listed?

_____

6. What is the highest level of education listed?

_____

SECTION 4

GETTING READY FOR INTERVIEWS

When Hector saw the newspaper ad, he called right away.

"My name is Hector Benitez," he said. "And I'm calling about the ad for a maintenance helper."

"Do you have any experience?" asked Ms. Jordan, a personnel employee.

"Yes, I'm the janitor for my apartment building," he said.

Ms. Jordan asked him a few more questions. Then she asked him to come for an interview the next day.

As he hung up the phone, Hector felt

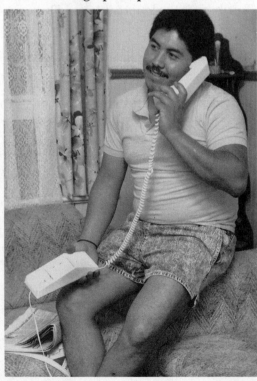

excited. He'd been looking for a job for almost two months. And this one looked good. He called his brother Luis.

"Luis," he said. "I have an interview tomorrow with a big company called Ambrose Products." He told Luis about the ad and his phone conversation.

"I've never gone on an interview before," he said. "What should I expect?"

"They will probably give you an application form to fill out first," Luis explained. "Look it over before you start writing on it."

"Why do I need to look it over?" Hector asked. "I've filled out application forms before."

"Yes, but each form is different," Luis said. "Also, tonight you should write down what other jobs you've had and where you went to school. Then take that information with you to the interview."

"OK," Hector said. "What's next?"

"After you fill out the application, someone will probably ask you questions such as why you left your last job or why you want this job. Prepare to answer questions like that tonight."

That evening Hector made notes for his job application. Then he thought about answers to the questions. He was ready to knock 'em dead!

Interviewing for Jobs

Hector was nervous about his job interview because he didn't know what to expect. He had never been on a formal job interview.

After he called his brother Luis, he felt better. That's because Luis helped Hector prepare for the interview. Luis told him what to expect and how to get ready ahead of time.

You can never know exactly what will happen on a job interview. But you can prepare yourself for situations that might arise.

An employer who invites you for an interview usually knows—from your application, resume, or application letter—that you have some qualifications for the job. Employers often interview the best qualified applicants. Therefore, you should feel confident in an interview because the employer obviously feels you're worth the time. Interviews give employers a chance to meet applicants and learn more about them.

Employers usually look carefully at applicants' **personal traits**, such as how well they listen and whether they display a positive attitude. You can show a positive attitude by being friendly and enthusiastic. The applicant who makes the best impression during an interview usually gets the job. You make a good impression by having a positive attitude and by being prepared.

"Doing Your Homework"

As part of your preparation for the interview, you should learn about the employer's business. This will make it easier for you to ask questions during the interview. It will also make it easier for you to show an employer that you're right for the job.

Before you go on an interview, try to find out:
♦ **what products or services the business provides**
♦ **how long the employer has been in business**

♦ **how many people are working there**
♦ **who its competitors are**

You can get this information from several sources. People who already work for a company can often give you information that you can't get anywhere else. The local Chamber of Commerce and the Better Business Bureau may have information about small businesses. Public libraries usually have several business directories that have plenty of information about companies, especially large ones. Also, the company's main office usually has literature about it. This is sometimes a part of the annual report. You can ask for a copy of it.

After you get information on the company, read it. Think about how, with your skills, you would fit into the business and contribute to its success. Then think about how you can convince the interviewer that you would be an asset to the business.

Before you go on an interview, find out as much as you can about the company. That way, you can figure out how to convince the interviewer that you're the right person for the job.

Find Out About the Job

If you are applying for a specific job, find out as much as you can about similar jobs before the interview. Look up the job in the *Occupational Outlook Handbook* or the *Dictionary of Occupational Titles*. Your instructor or program coordinator may have these books, or you can find them in the reference section of your public library.

When you find the job title, look for specific information, such as what the main duties are and what the primary work tasks involve (data, ideas, people, things). This kind of information can help you relate your background to the job that you're applying for.

Asking Questions

Before an interview, use the information you have found to prepare questions. This will show the interviewer that you prepared for the interview. Your questions will also help demonstrate your interest in the company and the job.

What kinds of questions should you ask?

♦ **Questions about the company.** Ask specific questions about the business. For example, if you're applying for a job in a restaurant, you might ask which days are the busiest or who manages the different shifts.

♦ **Questions about the responsibilities.** You should ask about specific duties—what you would be expected to do and where you would do it. For example, for a job as a delivery truck driver, you might ask how many deliveries you would make a day and in what neighborhood you would work.

♦ **Questions about the job opening.** If you don't already know the answers to the following questions, then you should ask:

When would I start?

What hours would I work?

Would I be expected to work any overtime?

What are the fringe benefits?

♦ **Questions about the hiring decision.** Be sure that you find out when the employer plans to make a decision. Ask whether you can call on a certain day to determine if a decision has been made.

Take a list of questions with you. Refer to the list. If, at the end of the interview, all of your questions have been answered, you can say so. This will let the interviewer know that you came prepared.

What Questions Would You Ask?

Get a copy of the local newspaper. Find a help-wanted ad that interests you in the classified section. Imagine that you have been invited to interview for that job. Make a list of five questions you would ask during the interview. List the questions in the order that you would ask them.

1. _____

   _____

2. _____

   _____

3. _____

   _____

4. _____

   _____

5. _____

   _____

What Questions Should You Expect?

When you go on an interview, you should be prepared to answer many questions about yourself and your qualifications. Some of those questions may be simple ones that you can answer quickly, perhaps with a yes or no. However, it is usually a good idea to provide some extra information when you answer. For example, you may be asked if you have ever operated a particular piece of equipment. A good way to answer would be: "Yes, I operated a crane on my last job. I ran the crane for three years and operated other large machinery, too." However, in an interview you may also be asked questions that are difficult to answer. The way you answer those questions may determine whether you get the job.

Before you go on an interview, you should think about how you would answer the following questions. You can't predict exactly which questions the interviewer will ask. But, if you think about all of the possibilities ahead of time, you will be prepared no matter what. Some of the most frequently asked questions include:

♦ Why should I hire you?
♦ What can you do for us?
♦ How dependable are you?
♦ What are your strengths?
♦ What are your weaknesses?
♦ Did you like school? What was your best subject?
♦ Why did you leave school before you graduated?
♦ Why are you applying for this job?
♦ Why do you think you can do this job?
♦ What did you like most (or least) about your last job?
♦ Why did you leave your last job? (Why do you want to leave the job you have now?)

♦ Have you ever been fired from a job? (If you say yes, be prepared to explain.)

The interviewer may also say, "Tell me something about yourself." This is a chance for you to spend a minute or two talking about your background and your skills. Be sure to describe how your experience and abilities relate to the job you're interviewing for. Don't respond to such a question by talking about your personal life, such as your family or hobbies.

Reviewing your resume and your responses to the questions you answered in Section 1 can help you answer these questions. Look over what you wrote about your interests, skills, talents, and work experience. Then think about how your background relates to the job. This can help you explain why you want the job and why you feel you're qualified for it. Also, think about how you can let the interviewer know that you are dependable. For example, do you usually get to work on time? Do you have a good attendance record at work?

What Answers Would You Give?

Use the help-wanted ad you found for the previous exercise. Once again, imagine that you are preparing for the interview. Practice by answering the following questions.

1. Why are you applying for this job?

_____

_____

2. Why do you think you can do this job?

_____

_____

3. What are your strengths?

_____

_____

4. What did you like most about your last job?

_____

_____

_____

Practice Aloud

After you think about how you would answer questions on an interview, practice answering them aloud. If you have a tape recorder, record your answers and play them back for yourself. As you listen, ask yourself:

♦ Did I speak clearly?

♦ Did I sound friendly and enthusiastic?

♦ Did I sound knowledgeable?

If your speech is unclear, try speaking more slowly and pronouncing words more carefully. If you didn't sound interesting and interested, keep practicing until you do.

Try to practice in front of a mirror, too. As you talk, watch your **body language**. Your body sends certain messages, which are based on your expressions, gestures, and posture. For example, if you slouch in your chair and avoid looking at the interviewer, you will send the message that you're uninterested. Eye contact is extremely important during an interview. Eye contact convinces people of your honesty and sincerity.

Work on showing your friendliness, confidence, and interest in what the interviewer is saying. Sit up straight and look the interviewer in the eye. Don't fidget or become distracted.

Answering Questions in a Positive Way

When some people see half a glass of water, they say the glass is half full. Others see the glass as half empty. People see the glass differently because of their attitude. Those with a positive attitude see the glass as half full. People with a negative attitude see it as half empty.

The way you see things and the way you explain what you see can make a difference in an interview. Employers want to hire workers who have a positive attitude.

You can learn how to express thoughts in a positive way. Instead of looking at a glass as half empty, look at it as half full. Employers like to see positive attitudes. The questions below are ones that you might be asked in an interview. After each question are two possible responses. One of the responses is better because it is stated in a more positive way.

Question: Why are you applying for this job?

♦ *Positive:* Because I'm interested in working for your company.

♦ *Negative:* Because I don't like the job I have now.

Question: Why did you leave school before you graduated?

♦ *Positive:* I had to get a job so I could help support my family.

♦ *Negative:* It was a waste of time.

Question: How did you get along with your last supervisor?

♦ *Positive:* We didn't always see eye to eye.

♦ *Negative:* I didn't like her.

Question: Why do you want to leave the job you have now?

♦ *Positive:* I want a more challenging job.

♦ *Negative:* It's boring.

Now look back at the questions on pages 39 and 40. Were your answers positive in tone or negative in tone?

If any of them were negative, try to answer them again in a more positive way.

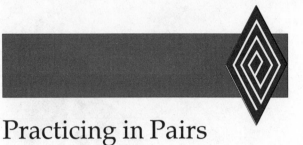

Practice Interviewing

Sometimes it's easier to ask and answer questions if you can practice with a friend or relative. Hector could have prepared for his interview at Ambrose Products by rehearsing the interview with his brother Luis.

Luis could have played the part of the interviewer. He could have asked Hector questions that a real interviewer might ask. Hector could have practiced giving answers. And he could have practiced asking questions.

Then Luis could have told Hector what kind of an impression he made. Did he stand, sit, and talk in a way that created a good impression? Were his speech and gestures appropriate?

If you don't have much experience interviewing, get some practice. Ask a friend or relative to play the role of the employer. Try to get someone who has been through job interviews and knows what they are like.

Dress the same way you would for a real interview. Greet the other person just as you would greet an employer. Shake hands firmly. Smile and look the other person in the eye. Give the answers you would give to the employer. Use the same gestures and the same tone of voice. Stand and sit straight.

Afterward, ask the other person what kind of impression you made. Was your clothing suitable? Did you give answers that would make an employer want to hire you? Did you have a friendly, enthusiastic, positive attitude? Ask the other person if he or she has suggestions for how you might make a better impression.

Practicing in Pairs

Practice interviewing for jobs with a friend, relative, or classmate. One person should play the role of the interviewer, and the other should play the role of the applicant. Then switch roles, so that each of you gets to play both parts.

When you are playing the part of the interviewer, ask questions such as those listed earlier. Then fill out the following form to let the applicant know what kind of impression he or she made. Include comments about why the applicant made a good impression or how the applicant could have made a better one.

	Excellent	Good	Fair
Appearance	_____	_____	_____
Posture	_____	_____	_____
Speech	_____	_____	_____
Attitude	_____	_____	_____
Questions Asked	_____	_____	_____
Answers to Questions	_____	_____	_____
Overall Impression	_____	_____	_____

Comments _____

_____

_____

When playing the part of the applicant, ask questions about the company, the responsibilities, the job opening, and the hiring decision. Answer the interviewer's questions as positively and confidently as you can.

Then fill out the following card to rate your own performance during the interview. Include an explanation of why you think you made a good impression or how you could have made a better one.

When you go for an interview, try to be as neat and well groomed as the person on the left. The other person's appearance is wrong. Can you explain why?

	Excellent	Good	Fair
Appearance	____	____	____
Posture	____	____	____
Speech	____	____	____
Attitude	____	____	____
Questions Asked	____	____	____
Answers to Questions	____	____	____
Overall Impression	____	____	____

Explanation _____

_____

_____

_____

_____

_____

Being Prepared to Take Tests

At your interview, the employer may want to test your aptitude, skills, personality traits, or general abilities. Employers use these tests to determine which applicants are best suited to jobs.

If you get nervous about taking tests, remember that test results can help you, too. If you are well suited to the job, the test results will help convince the employer of this. If you don't do well on the test, then the job may not be right for you.

A common employment test is an **aptitude test**. This test measures your natural abilities for performing or learning certain kinds of tasks. An aptitude test may measure your **potential** for doing well at clerical tasks, working with numbers, or using decision-making skills. If the test shows that you will probably develop those skills easily, then you have a high potential. Because aptitude tests measure your potential instead of your skills, you can't study for these tests.

Some aptitude tests involve writing answers to questions. Others require you to perform simple tasks. A test of your mechanical aptitude, for example, may require you to fit blocks into holes of matching shapes or put nuts and bolts together.

The General Aptitude Tests Battery (GATB) is a series of 12 aptitude tests— some of which involve paper and pencil and some of which involve tasks. Many employers use the GATB to test applicants.

Other types of tests may also be given. If you have applied for a job that requires clerical skills, such as secretary, word processor, file clerk, or bank teller, the employer could test your skills in those tasks. Depending on the job, you may be given a typing test or tests in filing, shorthand, or math.

An employer may give you a **personality test**, or **adjustment test**, to determine whether you have the personal traits that the job requires. Some employers also use these tests to decide whether applicants will fit into the workplace and get along well with co-workers. These tests show whether you are outgoing or quiet, how cooperative you are, whether you are aggressive, and much more.

Taking Employment Tests

Even though you can't study for most employment tests, keeping some tips in mind can help you when you are tested.

(continued)

- If you have a choice of where to sit when you take tests, choose a comfortable seat. It should be in a quiet spot with good light and a good work surface.
- Look over the test before you begin. Read the instructions, and ask for help if they are unclear.
- Find out whether the test is timed. If it is timed, ask how much time you will have and whether you will be warned when your time is nearly up. If the test includes several sections, find out if the sections will be timed separately.
- Find out how the test will be graded. Should you guess at answers you are unsure of or leave blanks?
- Ask what tools you can use. For example, find out if you can use a calculator or a scratch pad for solving problems. Use any tools you can, because they may help you work faster.
- Start the test as soon as you are told to do so. Stop when you are told that your time is up.
- Answer the questions in order.
- With a timed test, avoid spending too much time on any one question. If you can't answer a question right away, go on with the rest of the test and come back to that question later.
- If the answer sheet is one in which you fill in spaces or dots, don't skip *any* answers. Instead, put a tiny check by any answers that you're unsure of.
- If you have time, check your answers after you finish the test.
- On multiple choice questions, the first answer you put down is usually correct. Only change an answer if you are *sure* it is wrong.

Try These Test Questions

Employment tests that aren't skills-related may include any combination of the following:

♦ **true-or-false questions**
♦ **fill-in-the-blank questions**
♦ **questions that require you to answer in complete sentences or paragraphs**
♦ **multiple-choice questions**
♦ **questions that require you to put words or things in their proper order**

The following questions are ones that you might find on employment tests. Read the directions very carefully before you answer the questions.

Multiple Choice
Instruction: Write the letter of the correct answer in the space that follows the question.
Question: Which of the following is not an animal? _____
a. monkey   **b.** banana
c. giraffe   **d.** horse

Multiple Choice
Instruction: Use a pen or pencil to darken the slot marked by the letter that matches the letter of the correct answer.
Question: What is the difference between 158 and 73?
a. 128   **b.** 66   **c.** 85   **d.** 75
　a　　　　b　　　　c　　　　d
　| |　　　| |　　　| |　　　| |

Ordering Words
Instruction: List the following words in alphabetical order on the lines provided.

hardware   dinner   software
dress   telephone   diner
therapy   supplies   debate

Checking a Few More Details

There are a few details that you need to take care of before the interview.

♦ If you already have a job and you need to take time off for an interview, arrange to do so as early as possible. If you need to, plan for someone else to take your shift or do your work that day.

♦ Schedule a babysitter if you normally watch your children during the time of the interview. Have a backup babysitter in case one cancels at the last minute.

♦ A day or two before the interview, pick out the clothes that you plan to wear. (What to wear to an interview will be discussed in Section 5.) Check to make sure that the clothes you plan to wear are clean and ironed. Make sure that your shoes are polished. You don't want to worry about these details the morning of the interview.

♦ Arrange for dependable transportation to get to the interview. If you will use public transportation, check schedules in advance.

♦ If it's the first time you visit an employer, be prepared to fill out an application form. Prepare your notes ahead of time and put them with any other items you plan to take with you. Take a copy of your resume as well. You may be asked for one.

Planning Your Time

Arriving on time for a job interview is essential. In fact, it's a good idea to give yourself a few extra minutes, so you won't have to rush and so you'll arrive feeling calm.

You can make sure you arrive on time by figuring out how to get to the interview and how long it will take you to get there. Try to make the trip before you actually go for the interview. That way, you can be sure of the directions and how much time you need. When you make the trial trip, don't forget to take into account traffic, especially if you'll be going at a different time of day. And remember to allow time for walking to or from a bus stop or train station, finding a taxi, or parking your car.

To make sure you will be on time, take into account how much time you will need to:
♦ bathe and dress for the interview
♦ take a child to a babysitter or do other chores before you leave
♦ get to the interview a few minutes early so you will feel relaxed, not rushed

If an emergency occurs and you will be late to the interview or you have to cancel it, call the employer and explain. If possible, reschedule when you call.

Points to Remember

In this section, you learned some of the many things that you can do to prepare for an interview. Among the most important steps are the following:
♦ find out about the company you're applying to
♦ find out specific information about similar jobs
♦ prepare to ask questions about the company, the responsibilities, the job opening, and the hiring decision
♦ practice answering questions that interviewers frequently ask
♦ rehearse the interview with a friend or relative
♦ prepare to take different types of employment tests
♦ check to make sure other interview-related details are taken care of
♦ plan how much time you will need to get to the interview

✓ CHECKPOINT ✓

Word-Wise

Fill in the blanks below to complete the sentences. The answers are key terms introduced in this section.
1. An _____ _____ measures your natural abilities for performing or learning certain kinds of tasks.
2. The messages your movements send is your _____ _____.
3. Some tests measure your _____ , or the likelihood of your developing certain skills easily.

4. A _____ _____ is a test that determines whether you have the personal traits needed for the job.
5. Your _____ _____ include such things as how well you listen and your attitude.

Putting It to Work

You have been looking for a job for months. You have just been invited for an interview at a large company in your town.

Make a list of five things that you need to do in order to prepare for the interview.

1. _____
2. _____
3. _____
4. _____
5. _____

You Be the Judge

An employer whom you really want to work for has called and invited you for an interview the following day. You have accepted the invitation even though you normally work those hours, because you thought you could switch shifts with someone at work.

You tried to find someone to switch with you, but no one could. What would you do?

_____
_____
_____
_____
_____

Getting the Facts

Choose a business or company in your area that you would like to work for. Then choose a job you would like to have with that company.

Imagine that you have been invited for an interview there. Use the sources discussed in this section to find answers to the following questions.

1. What business or company did you choose? _____
_____

2. Where did you find answers to the questions about the business or company?
_____
_____

3. What products or services does the business provide? _____
_____

4. How long has the employer been in business? _____
_____

5. How many people work there? _____

_____

6. What job did you choose? _____

7. Where did you find the answers to the questions about the job? _____
_____
_____

8. What are the main duties of the job you chose? _____
_____
_____

9. How could you relate your background to the job? _____
_____
_____

10. Did you have trouble finding any of the answers? _____ If so, which ones?
_____
_____

11. Did you learn any other interesting facts about the job or business? _____ If so, what were they? _____
_____
_____

12. After reading the information about the business, would you still want to work there? _____ Why or why not?
_____
_____

13. After reading the information about the job, would you still want it? _____ Why or why not? _____
_____
_____

S ECTION 5

INTERVIEW DO'S AND DON'TS

Sue Miller reviewed the job application on her desk. She looked up and smiled at Robina Kaji, the young woman applying for the insurance clerk job.

"I see that you got your high school equivalency diploma last year. Why did you drop out?" Sue asked.

"My mother was sick, and I had to take care of her," Robina said. "After she got better, I worked and took classes at night to get my diploma."

Sue nodded. She liked Robina's attitude and her honesty.

"I see that you've taken classes since you got your diploma," Sue said. "Tell me about them."

"Well," Robina said, "I took courses in computer programming and beginning accounting. I liked the math. And I really enjoyed working with computers."

"Did you use computers in your last job?" Sue asked.

"No," Robina answered. "The clerks didn't have computers."

"What were your primary duties there?" Sue asked.

"I filed papers, answered phones, and typed letters," Robina replied.

"Did you like your job?" Sue asked.

"Yes, I liked it a lot. It was a good place to learn how an office runs," Robina said.

"Why did you leave?" Sue asked.

"Because I wanted a more challenging job where I could use my clerical skills *and* my computer skills," Robina said.

The two women talked about the type of tasks Robina would perform if she got the job as insurance clerk.

"That sounds like interesting work," Robina said. "Do you provide benefits?"

"Yes, we do," Sue answered.

They discussed the details of the benefits. Then Sue said, "Now I need to ask you to take a short clerical test."

Making a Good Impression

Robina made a good impression during her job interview with Sue Miller primarily because she:

♦ was well dressed and groomed
♦ had a positive attitude
♦ expressed herself well
♦ seemed honest
♦ answered Sue Miller's questions clearly and completely
♦ asked questions and showed her interest in the job

When you go on a job interview, it is important to make a good impression, as Robina did. You can do that by being prepared and by taking special care with your appearance.

Your appearance is very important in a job interview. It is an outward expression of how you feel about yourself. Interviewers will notice your personal **hygiene**, or good health and cleanliness, and the way you dress and are groomed. They will form an opinion of you based on those things. For example, if you wear sloppy clothes and don't brush your hair, people may think you are careless and disorganized at work, too.

When you dress for an interview, make sure your clothes are clean, ironed, and in good condition. If you're a man applying for an office or sales job, you should wear a suit or a jacket and tie. A woman should wear a dress or a skirt and blouse. If you're applying for a job that involves manual labor, you can dress less formally, but you should still look neat and clean.

Your grooming is as important as your clothing when you're trying to make a good impression. Here are some grooming tips that will help you make a good impression on an interviewer:

♦ Brush your teeth and be sure your breath is fresh.
♦ Bathe and use deodorant before you dress for the interview.

♦ Make sure your ears, hair, and fingernails are clean.
♦ Males should wear black, blue, or brown shoes that are clean, polished, and in good repair.
♦ If you're a woman, wear plain nylon stockings without patterns. If you're a man, wear socks of a solid dark color with no holes in them.
♦ If you use nail polish on your fingernails, be sure the polish is not chipped. Don't use flashy colors.
♦ If you use perfume, cologne, or makeup, use it lightly.
♦ Don't wear sunglasses, flashy jewelry, revealing clothing, or anything that might distract the interviewer. If you do, you might not be taken seriously.

In addition to clothing and grooming, your behavior affects the impression you make during an interview. Interviewers will closely watch the way you act and will interpret the unspoken messages you send. You are more likely to impress them if you're confident, enthusiastic, honest, and polite, and if you communicate the right messages through your body language. See the feature box on the next page for tips on using body language to make a good impression.

Interviewing Guidelines

There are many guidelines to follow when you go on an interview. The eight questions that follow concern some specific guidelines you should know. If you aren't sure about an answer, try to figure it out anyway. For some questions, both answers may be correct. These questions are so important that you will find the answers in the paragraph after number 8.

1. When you go on an interview, go
   _____
   a. alone   b. with your friends
2. When you arrive for an interview, give your _____
   to the receptionist or secretary.
   a. birth certificate   b. name
3. Expect to wait a few minutes in an outer office before meeting the interviewer. Use this time to_____.
   a. observe what goes   b. read the
      on in the office   newspaper
4. When you meet the interviewer, shake hands firmly. Take a seat only if it's offered. Don't _____.
   a. smoke   b. chew gum
5. Let the interviewer control the discussion. Never _____
   when the interviewer is talking.
   a. interrupt   b. listen
6. When it's your time to speak, use standard English. Don't use _____.
   a. slang   b. profanity
7. Avoid criticizing former employers and mentioning _____.
   a. your qualifications   b. personal
                                  problems
8. Try to let the interviewer bring up the subject of _____. If the interviewer doesn't, you can bring it up at the end of the interview.
   a. money   b. working hours

After you answer all the questions, check your answers against the following answers:
1. a ; 2. b ; 3. a ; 4. a & b ; 5. a ; 6. a & b ; 7. b ; 8. a .

Reread any of the questions you got wrong. If you don't understand why a question is answered the way that it is, ask your instructor or program coordinator to explain it to you.

What Does Your Body Language Say?

An interviewer's opinion of you is usually based on more than just the way you dress and groom yourself. His or her opinion is also based on your body language. During an interview, you can use the tips below to make a good impression.

♦ Look the interviewer in the eye.
♦ Shake hands firmly.
♦ Sit and stand still and straight, but not stiffly.
♦ Smile pleasantly.
♦ Don't yawn, look at your watch, or display other signs that tell the interviewer that you're either bored or rushed.
♦ Avoid touching or staring at anything on the interviewer's desk.
♦ Don't tap your fingers, bite your nails, or give any other sign that you're nervous or uncomfortable.

What Kind of Impression Would You Make?

Choose a job that you would like to have. Imagine that you are being interviewed for that job. Answer the following questions.
1. What is the job? _____
   _____
2. What would you wear to the interview?
   _____
   _____

3. What would you say to the receptionist or secretary? _____

_____

4. How would you greet the interviewer?

_____

_____

5. When would you bring up the subject of money and benefits?

_____

_____

Dealing with Difficult Situations

Some interviews are more difficult than others. You may be asked questions that you have a hard time answering. Or you may have to explain problems from your past.

For example, an interviewer may ask, "How much do you expect to earn?" It is best not to answer with a specific amount. If you do, you take the chance of naming an amount that is too high or too low.

The safest response to a question about pay might be: "I believe most people earn $7 to $10 an hour for this kind of work. How much is this company offering?" Or: "I've heard that the 'going rate' for this kind of work is anywhere from $300 to $400 a week, depending on the working conditions. What are the working conditions like here?" If you respond this way, you let the interviewer know that you are aware of the salary range, yet you don't name a specific amount. And both answers encourage the interviewer to give you the dollar amount first.

Interviews can be especially stressful if you have had problems that you don't want to discuss with employers. For example, an interviewer may notice a gap between jobs on your application form. When you are asked why you weren't working then, you may have to explain that you spent time in a rehabilitation center or in prison.

If you've had problems in the past, such as gaps in employment, being fired or arrested, or using alcohol or drugs, prepare for interviews by thinking about how you will explain them. If you're asked, you should describe the situation honestly and explain how you resolved your problem.

Many employers will hire qualified applicants who have had problems if the applicants seem to have recovered from their illnesses or learned from their mistakes. If you lie about a problem, however, the employer may learn the truth later and fire you for lying about your background.

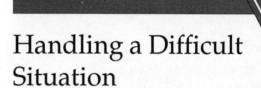

Handling a Difficult Situation

You can prepare for difficult situations by thinking about how you would handle them ahead of time. On a separate sheet of paper, describe a difficult situation that you may have to deal with. You can be honest—no one needs to read your response.

Think about how you would explain the situation to an interviewer. Then, on another sheet of paper, write what your explanation would be.

Your Rights as an Applicant

You have learned that you will be better prepared for an interview if you know what to expect. The same holds true for knowing what *shouldn't* take place in an interview.

Employers should not treat you differently because of your race, religion, national origin, ancestry, age, or sex. When employers do that, they're discriminating against you. Employers should not **discriminate** against a person with a disability either. The decision to hire should be based on the person's ability to perform the job. There are federal and state laws that protect people from all these types of discrimination.

Even though laws protect you against discrimination, it is still possible that an interviewer or an application form will request information that could be used to discriminate against you. The feature on this page shows some examples of these types of questions. What should you do if you are asked these questions? Keep in mind that if you answer the questions, the employer may discriminate against you. However, if you refuse to answer the questions, the employer may not hire you. Either way, however, there is something that you can do to take action against suspected discrimination.

If you feel you were not hired because of discrimination—or because you refused to answer discriminatory questions—you can contact the nearest office of the federal **Equal Employment Opportunity Commission** (EEOC). This agency enforces federal **civil rights** laws. Civil rights are rights granted to U.S. citizens by the U.S. Constitution. You can also contact your state's Civil Rights Commission, which enforces state laws against discrimination.

Either agency will listen to your side of the story and then will listen to the employer's side. If the agency finds that the employer violated antidiscrimination laws, you may get the job you were denied.

If you believe that an employer has discriminated against you, you can also get help from private organizations. One such group is the American Civil Liberties Union (ACLU). Lawyers from this organization will represent people who claim they have been denied the rights granted to them by the U.S. Constitution.

Think Carefully Before You Answer

During an interview, you may think that you have to answer every question you're asked. However, unless a question relates directly to the job you're seeking, an employer has no right to ask it. In fact, some questions may even break federal or local laws.

If an interviewer asks you any of the following questions, or any other question that seems too personal, you may want to refuse to answer it. Or you could ask how the information relates to the job, then decide whether to answer it.

♦ How old are you?
♦ Are you single or married?
♦ Do you plan to marry? Do you plan to have children?
♦ Do you have children?
♦ Do you have child care arranged? What would you do if one of your children were sick on a workday?
♦ Do you have any physical handicaps?
♦ What race are you?
♦ What country were you born in?
♦ Do you live by yourself?
♦ Do you drink alcohol or use other drugs?

How Would You Answer This?

You are being interviewed for a job. You have answered questions about your qualifications. And you have asked questions about the job. Then the interviewer asks you how old you are. What would you say? _____

_____

_____

After that, the interviewer asks if you're single. What would you say? _____

_____

_____

Read Carefully Before You Sign

You need to beware of more than just questions in an interview. An employer or an employment agency may ask you to sign a **contract**. If you are asked to sign a written agreement, make sure that you understand exactly what you're signing.

♦ Read the contract carefully. Don't take the interviewer's word for what the contract says.

♦ If there's something in a contract that you don't understand, have a lawyer read it and explain it to you before you sign it.

♦ Be sure you understand your own responsibilities as well as the responsibilities of the employer or agency. If you sign a contract with an employment agency, for example, the contract should spell out who pays the agency's fee if the agency finds you a job. A contract with an employer should list what your duties, wages, and benefits will be.

Ending the Interview

The way that an interview ends can leave a lasting impression on an interviewer. If possible, you should try to watch for signs that the interview is coming to an end.

An interviewer might signal the end by closing the folder that contains your application or by pushing back his or her chair. After one of these signals, ask your final questions or make a closing statement. And be brief. You can spoil an otherwise good impression by taking too much of the interviewer's time.

Before you leave, try to get all of the basic information you need to make a decision about whether or not you would want the job. If you haven't discussed salary or benefits yet, ask about them now.

If an interviewer tells you at the end of the interview that you won't be offered the job, try to find out why. You may learn about something you did wrong. Or you may learn that your qualifications weren't quite right for the job. Either way, this information can help you when you go on interviews for other jobs in the future.

If the interviewer ends the interview by offering you the job, you may want to ask for some time—perhaps a day or two—to make a decision. However, if you're absolutely certain, you may want to accept the offer immediately or turn it down.

Don't be surprised if a decision isn't made at the end of the interview. Most interviews end that way. Moreover, some job candidates must undergo two and even three rounds of interviews. However, if the interviewer doesn't tell you when the hiring decision will be made, ask about it. You also may want to ask if the company will notify you when a decision has been made.

At the end of every interview, thank the interviewer for his or her time. If you have already decided that you wouldn't accept the job if it were offered to you, tell the interviewer before you leave. You don't have to explain your reasons unless the interviewer asks you for an explanation.

If you're very interested in the job, say so. That way the interviewer will know where you stand. And it's likely that your enthusiasm will be remembered.

Do your best to end interviews on a positive note. How can you tell this woman has a positive attitude?

Evaluating an Interview

After any job interview you have, it's a good idea to **evaluate** your performance. If you do that, you can determine what you did well and what you need to improve for future interviews.

You can use the questions below to help you evaluate job interviews that you go on in the future.

♦ Was I on time for the interview? If not, how could I have avoided being late?

♦ Did I tell the interviewer everything I wanted him or her to know about me? If not, what else should I have said?

♦ Did I volunteer any negative information about myself? If so, how could I have avoided it?

♦ Did I find out everything I needed to know

about the job? If not, what else should I have asked?

♦ Did the interviewer ask questions that I was unprepared to answer? If so, how can I be prepared next time?

♦ What kind of overall impression did I make? What might I have done to make a better impression?

♦ Did I end the interview on a positive note? If not, how could I do so in the future?

Following Up on the Interview

Immediately after the interview, send a brief letter to thank the interviewer for his or her time. Type the letter on plain 8 1/2-by-11-inch paper, and address it to the person

SAMPLE THANK-YOU LETTER

18 Hoffman Drive
St. Paul, MN 55214
August 13, 199X

Nancy Chang
Assistant Manager
Wilson's Department Store
4500 Estates Boulevard
St. Paul, MN 55201

Dear Ms. Chang:

Thank you for the time and consideration shown to me
during my interview for the salesclerk job on Friday,
August 10.

I am quite interested in the job and I feel confident
I could handle the responsibilities. I would like you
to consider me a serious applicant for the position.

I look forward to hearing from you in the near
future.

Sincerely,

Melanie Harris

Melanie Harris

Writing a thank-you letter is an effective way to follow up on an interview.

who interviewed you. Be sure to spell the interviewer's name correctly. If you're not sure of the spelling, call the company. Check your letter to make sure it is error free.

If you want the job, say so. If you don't want the job, explain why and thank the interviewer. It's always good to end on a positive note. Other jobs may become available in the same company.

If the interviewer has given you an application form to take home, complete it and return it with your thank-you letter. Also send along any other papers the interviewer requested, such as a copy of your high school diploma. Don't send originals.

If you haven't heard from the interviewer after one week, call and find out if the job has been filled. Wait longer if the interviewer said it would take more time to make a decision.

When you call, you may be told that the job has been filled. You can try to find out why you didn't get the job. Or the interviewer may tell you that no decision has been made. Even so, your call won't hurt your chances of getting the job. Your call will simply remind the employer of your interest in working for the company. And your call will keep your name in the interviewer's mind for this job or another one in the future.

Writing a Thank-You Letter

Choose a job that you're interested in. Suppose that a man named Frank Wilson interviewed you for that job today. On a separate sheet of paper, write a thank-you letter to Mr. Wilson at the company at 59 Second Street in your town. Refer to the letter on page 54 as an example.

Points to Remember

In this section, you learned that there are many things to do when you interview for a job. Among the most important are the following:
♦ make a good impression by taking special care with your appearance and behavior
♦ be prepared to answer difficult questions
♦ be informed about your legal rights as an applicant
♦ know when and how to end an interview
♦ follow up on the interview

✓ C H E C K P O I N T ✓

Word-Wise

Fill in the blanks below to explain some important points about interviewing. The answers are key terms introduced in this section.

Employers cannot _____ against applicants because of their race, religion, national origin, or sex. If employers do that, they deny you your _____.

If you feel you have been treated unfairly, you can contact the federal _____

_____ ,

which enforces federal laws. Any employer may legally ask you to sign a _____ , which is a written agreement that spells out what is required of both you and the employer. After every interview, you should _____ your performance.

Putting It to Work

Your nineteen-year-old sister has an interview tomorrow. She has come to you for advice on how to dress and groom herself for the interview. On the lines below, write what you would say to her.

_____
_____
_____
_____
_____
_____

You Be the Judge

You were interviewed two weeks ago for a job that you want, and you still haven't heard from the employer. The interviewer told you that she would make a decision about the job within a week or two. What would you do?

_____
_____
_____
_____
_____

Getting the Facts

Let's say you were discriminated against in an interview. You're not sure whether the interviewer violated a federal or state law.

What agency would you contact to find out if it was a federal law?

_____

Now find the address and telephone number of that agency.
Address: _____
Phone number: _____
Where did you find that information? _____
_____

What agency would you contact to find out if it was a state law? _____
_____

Now find the address and telephone number of that agency.
Address: _____
Phone number: _____
Where did you find that information? _____
_____

What private organization could you contact to get help defending your rights?
_____

Now find the address and telephone number of that organization.
Address: _____
Phone number: _____
Where did you find that information? _____
_____

If you couldn't find all of the information above, list the sources you checked: _____
_____
_____

MAKING THE RIGHT CHOICE

"You look pretty happy," Aunt Ellen remarked, smiling at her niece.

"I am," Nancy said. "I got two job offers today. Both are sales jobs in clothing stores. One's at TJ's downtown. And the other's at Fashion Hut at the mall."

"That's great," Aunt Ellen said. "Do you know which one you're going to take?"

"No," Nancy replied. "I've been thinking about it, but I'm not sure yet."

"Which one do you think you would like better?" Aunt Ellen asked.

"I like both of them equally," Nancy said. "And they both pay the same."

"It sounds like a tough choice," Aunt Ellen said. "But there are other things to think about, too."

"Like what?" Nancy asked.

"How far would you have to travel to each job? And how much would your transportation cost?" Aunt Ellen asked.

"Well," Nancy said, "I could take the bus downtown to TJ's. But I would have to drive to the mall. The bus would definitely be cheaper than driving."

"You have to consider the hours you would work, too," Aunt Ellen said.

"At Fashion Hut I would have to work three nights a week. TJ's is only open Wednesday night, so I'd only work there one night a week," Nancy said.

"Do you get similar fringe benefits at both shops?" Aunt Ellen asked.

"Yes," Nancy said. "They both provide medical insurance, paid vacations, and paid sick days."

"Are there any differences between the benefits?" Aunt Ellen asked.

"I don't know," Nancy replied. "I'll have to look at the information I got in the interviews. Once I've read through everything, I'll make a decision."

"Good luck," Aunt Ellen said. "And let me know what you decide."

Is This Job Right for You?

Nancy's aunt helped her recognize important differences between the two jobs she was offered. By evaluating those differences, Nancy discovered what her job **preferences** and values were. For instance, Nancy preferred one location over another. And she preferred the job in which she would work fewer nights.

Similar jobs may seem the same on the surface but may differ in important ways. If you are offered a job, how do you decide whether it is right for you?

To choose the right job, you should be aware of your job preferences. If you know what to expect before you take a job, then your chances of being satisfied with the job are much greater. Ask yourself these questions to evaluate a job and decide if it's right for you:

♦ **Where is the job located?** How will I get to and from work, and how much will it cost?

It's important to weigh the pros and cons of a job *before* you take it.

♦ **What hours would I have to work?** Will I work regular hours? Will I work nights, weekends, or overtime?

♦ **How much does the job pay?** What is the salary, and will it cover my expenses?

♦ **What benefits come with the job?** Will the company provide medical insurance, paid vacation, and other benefits?

♦ **How much money would the job cost me?** What would I have to spend on transportation, food, clothing, and other costs?

♦ **What are the working conditions?** Would I be working indoors or outdoors, alone or with people?

♦ **What future does the job offer?** Are there chances for learning, training, or advancement?

Few jobs will satisfy all of your job preferences. You probably won't find a high-paying job that offers training and a company child care center within walking distance of your home. You will usually have to make **trade-offs** when you evaluate a job. That means you will have to give up some things you want in order to have others. The key is to give up the things that are least important to you.

Nancy's sister, Christine, decided to go back to work when her children started school. Christine's preferences for a secretarial job included working close to home, working flexible hours, and having enough paid sick days. She was offered a job with flexible hours and three weeks of paid sick days a year. She decided to take the job even though it wasn't close to home. That's because Christine's other preferences were more important to her than working close to home. She felt that she needed the flexible hours and paid sick days so she could take care of her children when they needed her.

In this section, you will take a closer look at each of the questions above. By doing so, you will discover which preferences mean the most to you. And you will learn which preferences you're willing to trade off.

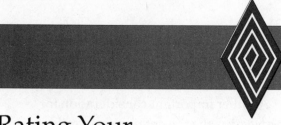

Rating Your Preferences

On the lines below, list the five preferences that matter most to you. You can use the ones listed below, or you can come up with your own. Either way, be sure to put them in order of importance, with number 1 being the most important and number 5 being the least important.

Convenient location
Regular hours
High salary
Good benefits
Low work expenses
Good working conditions
Good chance for advancement

1. _____
2. _____
3. _____
4. _____
5. _____

Where Is the Job Located?

Nancy decided that being able to take the bus to work was important to her. She knew that she could borrow her parents' car for awhile but that she would eventually have to buy a car. She didn't think she could afford to buy her own car. For Nancy, the job's convenient location was a preference.

A job's location is an important consideration. Most people want to work at a place that isn't too far away from home and that isn't too difficult to get to. For example, if you live in the country or in the suburbs, you may not want to take the time to travel back and forth to a job in the city.

The amount of time you spend **commuting** often depends on the type of transportation you use to get to work. Your time will vary depending on whether you drive, walk, ride a bike, or take a bus or train. However, the location of the job usually determines how you can get there. For example, Nancy couldn't take a bus to the mall because it wasn't on a bus route.

When you start looking for a job, therefore, you need to ask yourself what kinds of dependable transportation are available to you. Do you already have a reliable car? Is there a bus or train stop near your home? Does the public transportation near you go directly to a business area, or would you have to transfer to another bus or train? Can you walk or ride a bike to work? In bad weather, could you find other means of transportation?

If you're not sure what public transportation is available, you should find out. Get schedules and route maps for the trains, buses, or subways near your home. You can get them from your local or county transportation department. See which trains, buses, or subways stop near your home. And find out what areas they travel to.

When you apply for a job, consider whether you could use public transportation to get there. Is the job in an area that is convenient to get to? Do the transportation schedules fit in with the hours you would be working?

You also need to consider the cost of transportation to and from a job. Find out how much the train or bus fare would cost you each day. Remember that weekly or monthly passes save you money. If the job isn't near public transportation, you need to consider how much it would cost you to drive. When you figure out the cost of driving, be sure to include gas, tolls, parking, repairs, and insurance. Figuring out the cost of transportation is important. If a job costs too much to get to, it may not be worth taking.

Reading a Bus Schedule

Schedules for public transportation can be very confusing. To get practice, read the one below and answer the questions that follow.

TO DOWNTOWN (CENTRAL AVE) WEEKDAYS

1ST AVE	SPRING ST	WELLS AVE	CENTRAL AVE
7:15 A.M.	7:45	7:58	8:15
7:50 A.M.	8:20	8:33	8:50
8:15 A.M.	8:45	8:58	9:15

FROM DOWNTOWN (CENTRAL AVE) WEEKDAYS

CENTRAL AVE	WELLS AVE	SPRING ST	1ST AVE
4:45 P.M.	5:16	5:28	5:45
5:20 P.M.	5:51	6:03	6:20
6:15 P.M.	6:41	6:53	7:08

NO SERVICE SATURDAYS, SUNDAYS, AND HOLIDAYS

Imagine that you live near the bus stop on Spring Street. You are offered a job downtown on Central Avenue. You would work from 9 A.M. to 5 P.M. on weekdays.

1. What time would you have to catch the bus to get to work by 9 A.M.? _____
2. How much time would it take you on the bus to travel to work? _____
3. What time would you get off the bus on your trip home? _____
4. If the job required you to work some hours on weekends, what would you do?

_____

What Hours Would You Work?

Another important consideration for Nancy was the time of day she would work. She didn't want to work many nights, as she would have been required to do at Fashion Hut.

Working hours are an important consideration for most people. Some people want to work regular daytime hours because they need to coordinate their schedules with spouses, school or child care facilities, or available transportation. Some people look for hours that will allow them to pursue outside interests or activities, such as attending school. Some need to work hours that will allow them to take care of family members.

For example, Don wanted a night job so he could stay home during the day to care for his three young children. His wife worked half-days, and they couldn't afford to pay a baby-sitter, so Don got a job driving a bus at night.

Some companies provide flexible working hours to accommodate employees who have different schedules. Companies that offer **flextime**, for example, allow employees to choose their own working hours (within certain limits) provided that they work the required number of hours each week.

Other companies have **shift work**. Shift work is common in industries that operate 24 hours a day. Employees usually work an eight-hour shift. These shifts may be early in the day, late at night, or at times in between. Shift work is most common in manufacturing, transportation, and some service jobs, such as in hotels, airlines, and hospitals. Shift work is helpful to people who need time to do other things. For example, Sherry goes to school in the morning. Her evening job as a hotel receptionist gives her the time she needs for her schoolwork.

Some people work flexible hours by taking part in **job sharing**. Job sharing involves two people sharing the same job. Each person works part-time. Together, they hold down one full-time job. This arrangement requires a lot of cooperation between people.

Another point to consider when you evaluate jobs is whether you will have to work overtime. Some companies expect their employees to put in extra time whenever necessary. Before you accept a job, find out if you'll be expected to work overtime and how much you will be paid when you do.

How Much Money Will You Take Home?

The amount of money a job pays, the **salary**, is one of the most important things to consider about any job. When you find out a salary, make sure that the amount the employer quotes is **gross pay**. Gross pay is the pay you earn before deductions are taken out. Your **net pay,** or **take-home pay,** is the amount of money you take home.

The largest deductions taken out of your gross pay are for federal and state **income tax**. These are taxes that you must pay on your income. In general, the more money you make, the more federal and state tax you pay. However, you pay less tax if you have children or other family members to support.

Most people must pay between 20 and 25 percent of their salaries for various deductions. If an employer tells you what your gross pay will be, subtracting 20 to 25 percent from it will give you a good idea of how much pay you will take home.

Paying Workers Differently

Employers pay their workers in a variety of ways. The most common include:

♦ **Hourly pay.** In this situation, you are paid a fixed amount for each hour you work. You may have to punch a **time clock** when you begin and end work each day.

♦ **A straight salary.** With a salary, the amount of money you make may be quoted as a weekly, monthly, or yearly figure.

♦ **Tips.** Some service workers, such as waiters and waitresses and taxi drivers, receive tips from their customers. Because of the tips, these workers often get lower hourly wages than those of employees in other jobs. Even though tips are not part of a regular salary, workers must still report tips and pay income tax on them.

♦ **Commission.** In many sales jobs, employees are paid a salary plus a **commission**. This is a percentage of the amount of money the salesperson earns for the company. Some salesworkers receive no salary. They are paid a commission only.

If you find that most or all of your pay for a job will be in the form of tips or a commission, keep in mind that the amount you earn may vary greatly from one week to another. One week may be busy, whereas another may be slow. Some workers like being on commission or receiving tips, since the more customers you serve, the higher your earnings can be.

Deductions from Gross Pay

All workers must have certain deductions taken from their gross pay. The most common ones include:

♦ **Federal income tax.** The federal government takes a certain percentage of your gross pay to pay your yearly federal tax.

♦ **State and local income taxes.** Many states and some cities tax the incomes of people who live or work there. Depending on where you live and work, you will probably have to pay a percentage of your gross pay for these yearly taxes.

♦ **Social Security.** This is usually listed as FICA on payroll stubs. You pay a percentage of your salary to this fund that provides old-age insurance and benefits to covered workers and their survivors.

♦ **Unemployment insurance.** A small amount is deducted from your gross pay and put into a fund that you can draw from if you become unemployed.

♦ **Disability insurance.** A small amount is deducted from your gross pay so you will have insurance benefits if you become ill or disabled and can't work.

♦ **Union dues.** These dues may be deducted from the gross pay of workers who belong to a particular union.

♦ **Retirement payments.** Some employers deduct money from workers' gross pay to pay for part of their pension plan.

♦ **Medical benefits payments.** Some employers deduct money from workers' gross pay to pay for part of the medical benefits for employees and, possibly, the employees' families.

Figuring Out Pay

Imagine that you've found several ads in the newspaper for jobs that interest you. Before you answer any of the ads, you want to figure out how much your gross pay and your take-home pay would be for each job.

Calculate the pay for the three jobs that follow. Use the figure of 20 percent as the deduction to calculate the amount of take-home pay.

Job #1:
It pays $7.50 an hour for a 40-hour work week. The weekly gross pay would be

_____.

The weekly take-home pay would be

_____.

Job #2:
It pays $18,200 per year (a year is 52 weeks). The weekly gross pay would be

_____.

The weekly take-home pay would be

_____.

Job #3:
It pays $8.50 an hour for a 35-hour work week. The weekly gross pay would be

_____.

The weekly take-home pay would be

_____.

What Are the Company Benefits?

Most full-time workers are paid more than money for their work. They also receive **fringe benefits**. These forms of payment decrease workers' expenses and improve their morale. For example, many companies provide medical insurance for their employees. Medical insurance helps employees pay their medical bills.

When a company provides you with medical benefits, you may save hundreds of dollars a year in health insurance expenses. That's why it's important to consider the value of fringe benefits when you're comparing different jobs.

People's needs for fringe benefits differ greatly. Remember Nancy's sister, Christine? To her, paid sick days were a very important benefit. That benefit might not be important to Nancy, since she's rarely sick and she doesn't have to care for anybody else.

When you evaluate a job, you should learn all about the fringe benefits. Ask yourself how valuable these benefits will be for you. Decide which benefits are most important to you.

Learning About Benefits

Fringe benefits vary greatly from one company to another. The most common ones include:

♦ **Paid vacation.** The company pays you for a certain number of days each year that you are on vacation. Most often, an employee is eligible for a vacation of one to two weeks after one year from the date of hire.

♦ **Paid sick time.** The company pays you for a certain number of days each year that you are out sick.

♦ **Paid personal time.** The company pays you for a certain number of days each year when you're absent from work taking care of personal business.

♦ **Medical/dental insurance.** The company contributes to a health insurance plan that covers hospital, doctor, and dental bills for you and your family.

♦ **Life insurance.** The company provides an insurance policy for its employee in the event of the employee's death. If you die while employed by the company, the insurance money is paid to the person you have chosen, or your **beneficiary**.

♦ **Disability insurance.** The company provides insurance for you in case you become seriously ill or disabled and can't work.

♦ **Maternity/paternity leave.** The company pays your salary for a certain time period while you are home with

(continued)

your newborn or newly adopted child.

♦ **Pension plan.** The company sets aside money for you that you can collect when you retire.

♦ **Child care.** The company pays for all or part of the child care costs for its workers who have children, or the company has an on-site child care facility.

Rating Fringe Benefits

On the lines below, list the five fringe benefits that matter most to you. You can use benefits from the list in the feature, or you can add benefits of your own. Either way, be sure to put them in order of importance, with number 1 being the most important and number 5 being the least important.

1. _____

2. _____

3. _____

4. _____

5. _____

How Much Money Will You Spend to Work?

When figuring out what they will earn at certain jobs, many people don't consider how much money the job will cost them. No matter what job you take, you will have to spend some money to work.

You already learned that transportation can be a big expense when you work. You may also have to buy special clothing, tools, or equipment. Some employees, such as nurses, security officers, or food workers, require special uniforms. If you work in an office, you may have to conform to certain dress codes. Salespeople may have to have their own cars. All of these expenses can reduce the amount of money you have left to spend.

Food is also a job-related expense. The law says that full-time workers must have a meal-time break if they work more than four hours. You need to consider where you will eat that meal and approximately how much your food will cost you each week. For example, does the company have a lunchroom where you can eat a lunch you bring from home? Or would you have to buy your lunch each day? How much would eating out cost you?

Workers who have children may have to spend money for babysitters or child care while they work. If you have children who will need to be cared for while you work, you must calculate how much child care will cost. Some large companies offer child care services for their employees' children. But most companies don't provide such services.

There are other job-related expenses you may have to consider. If you work in a state or city other than the one you live in, you may have to pay a nonresident income tax. This out-of-state tax may not be deducted from your pay, so you may have to set aside money to pay this income tax each year. Similarly, if your union dues or pension plan payments aren't deducted from your gross pay, you may have to pay those fees.

The following chart will help you figure out how much money your job will cost you. When considering a job, write down approximately how much money you will have to spend per month on each of the items listed. Then add the dollar amounts to figure out about how much it will cost to work at that job.

ITEM	MONTHLY DOLLAR AMOUNT
Transportation	
Clothing	
Tools	
Equipment	
Food	
Child care	
Out-of-state taxes	
Union dues	
Pension plan	
Other	
TOTAL	

Other Factors to Consider

When you evaluate jobs, there are a few other factors to consider. Some of the most important factors include the working conditions, the specific work tasks, and the advancement possibilities.

Each job that you consider taking is tied to certain kinds of working conditions. You need to look at all of those working conditions before you can decide if the job would be right for you.

You can begin to evaluate working conditions by asking yourself the following questions. These questions will help you figure out what kind of environment you would prefer working in.

♦ Would I rather work indoors or outdoors?

♦ Would I rather work alone, with a few other people, or with a large group of people?

♦ Would I rather sit or stand all day?

♦ Would I rather work under close supervision or independently?

- Do I mind working in a hectic and noisy environment?
- Do I mind getting dirty while I work?
- Do I prefer routine schedules, or do I prefer variety?

Working environments are influenced by the work tasks being performed in particular jobs. For example, if you're a welder, then you'll probably work in a noisy, dirty environment. However, the environment and the tasks may vary from job to job. Depending on the job, the welder may work indoors or outdoors, alone or with people, sitting or standing, doing routine tasks or a variety of tasks.

Because of those differences, it's important to get all the details about a job before you evaluate it. Only then can you decide if the job would be right for you.

If you like the working conditions of a job, then you should consider what kind of future the job would offer. You probably want to have a better job with better pay sometime in the future. One of the most effective ways to achieve this goal is to work for a business or company that promotes its valuable workers.

When you apply for a job, try to find out what you can look forward to with the company. You might ask whether you would have the opportunity to get further training or to learn new skills. The more training and skills you acquire, the more valuable you will be to employers. And the more valuable you are, the better your chances are for getting raises and promotions.

When you talk to employers, don't be afraid to ask direct questions. For example, you might ask: Are employees encouraged to take on more responsibilities? Are people frequently promoted in their jobs with the company? Are raises and promotions awarded to outstanding workers? By asking these questions, you will show the employer that you care about your own future. You will also show that you're interested in a future with the company.

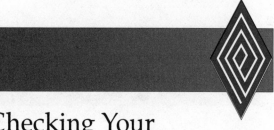

Checking Your Ratings

At the beginning of the section, you rated the five preferences that mattered most to you. Reread the list you wrote and answer the questions below.

1. After reading the information in this section, would you change any of your ratings now? _____

   If so, what would you change? _____

   _____

   _____

2. If you changed any of your ratings, explain why. _____

   _____

   _____

3. If you didn't change any of your ratings, explain why. _____

   _____

   _____

Points to Remember

In this section, you learned that there are many factors to consider when you evaluate and choose a job. Some of the most important include:
- the transportation you would use to get to work and its cost
- the hours you would work
- the salary you would be paid
- the benefits you would receive
- the money your job would cost you
- the working conditions
- the possibilities for future advancement

✓ CHECKPOINT ✓

Word-Wise

Fill in the blanks below to complete the sentences. The answers are key terms introduced in this section.

1. Some companies offer flexible working hours, or _____.

2. The money you earn *before* deductions have been taken out is your _____

   _____.

3. Sometimes two employees work part-time in the same job, which is called _____

   _____.

4. *After* deductions have been taken out, the pay you get is your _____,

   or your _____.

5. When you give up one thing to have another, you are making a _____.

Putting It to Work

You have been offered two similar jobs. List five factors that you would have to consider carefully when evaluating the jobs.

1. _____
2. _____
3. _____
4. _____
5. _____

You Be the Judge

You have been offered two similar jobs. They are alike in some ways: they're about the same distance from where you live and the benefits are similar. The main differences are these:

♦ Job #1 pays $8 an hour but doesn't offer any future advancement possibilities. You would not have to work nights or weekends.

♦ Job #2 pays $7 an hour but offers many chances for future training and advancement. You would have to work one night a week and every other Saturday.

What would you do? Explain your answer.

_____

_____

_____

_____

Getting the Facts

Look through the newspaper for two help-wanted ads that interest you. Make sure these ads list the employers' addresses. Think about how you would get to each job. Then answer the following questions.

	Job 1	Job 2
1. Could you take public transportation?	_____	_____
2. If so, what type would you take?	_____	_____
3. What would the fare be each day?	_____	_____
4. If you were to drive to work, how many miles is the trip each day?	_____	_____
5. About how much money would you spend driving?	_____	_____
6. Could you carpool with others?	_____	_____

7. Which job would be the better commute?

_____

SECTION 7

ADAPTING TO THE WORK WORLD

"Leroy, are you home?" Selena called out as she walked in the front door.

"I'm in the kitchen," Leroy answered.

Selena took off her coat and walked into the kitchen. "Hi," she said. "How are you?"

"Hi, Mom. I'm fine. How about you? How was your first day?"

"It was pretty good," Selena said, as she smiled. She picked up a spoon to taste the chili Leroy was making for dinner. "And this is great," she added.

"Thanks," Leroy said. "But I want to hear what happened today."

"Well, let's see," Selena said. "Everybody was really friendly. My boss, Ms. Cruz, showed me where everything was and how to work the copy machines, the fax machine, and the phones. I have my own desk and my own telephone extension. I'll write my number down in the book."

"Did you do much work today?" Leroy asked.

"I spent most of the morning with Ms. Cruz," she said. "But this afternoon I did a lot of work."

"Do you like it better than watching kids in the neighborhood?" Leroy asked.

"Yes," Selena replied. "I like it better. It's much more exciting. The office is really busy. The phones are constantly

ringing. I think it's going to be very challenging organizing the filing system."

"What are the people like?" Leroy asked.

"They're really nice," Selena answered. "Ms. Cruz introduced me to everybody. And all afternoon people kept asking me if I needed help."

"I'm so glad you like it," Leroy said.

"So am I," Selena said. "After babysitting for so many years, I wasn't sure that I would like being in an office. But it's really a welcome change. Now, let's have some of that chili while it's still hot."

Making Adjustments

Selena was excited and happy as she thought back on her first day at the office. She had arrived at 9 A.M., well rested and ready to get to work. She had used her time wisely—watching, listening, and learning a lot about her job and about the company.

As she had expected, the busy office environment was very different from the homes where she used to babysit. Naturally, she still felt nervous when she thought about all the tasks ahead of her. But she was confident that she would soon catch on to the new job routines. That evening, Selena sat quietly by herself and reviewed the day's events.

When you begin a new job, you may find that your first day is similar to Selena's. She enjoyed her first day and looks forward to going back to work. Even though Selena feels that way, she will still go through an **adjustment period**. During that time, she will learn to adapt to new routines and new people.

If you don't feel like Selena did after your first day at a new job, don't worry. Many people experience anxiety on a job until they adjust. Change can be very difficult. That's why you shouldn't quit a new job until you've given yourself a few weeks to adjust to it.

Like Selena, your first day will probably begin with a discussion between you and your boss. Your boss will explain the specific tasks you're responsible for. And you will ask questions so that you understand exactly how to do things.

At Selena's office, her boss gave her a written **job description** that listed all of her responsibilities and everyday duties. Selena and her boss reviewed the description together, and Ms. Cruz answered Selena's questions. If you are given a job description, it's a good idea to go over it in detail with your boss.

Some large companies give new employees an **orientation day**. During that day, employees learn about the job and the company. This usually takes place before an employee's first working day.

No matter which way you spend your first day, try to find out what you're expected to accomplish each day. This will help you avoid misunderstandings and mistakes in the future. Ask questions, such as:

♦ Who will evaluate my work? Who will train me?

♦ Will anyone besides my supervisor give me work? Will anyone be working with me?

♦ Where should I do my work?

♦ What equipment will I have to use? Where are supplies kept, and how do I get them?

♦ What hours should I work? What time should I check in and out? Should I punch a time clock?

♦ When should I take lunch and breaks? How much time do I get for lunch and breaks? Where can I take them?

When you start a new job, you might be given a tour of the workplace. A tour can help you learn the layout of the place and the duties of the different workers.

Most new employees spend some time the first day meeting co-workers. When Ms. Cruz took Selena on a tour of the office, Selena met more than a dozen people. She wondered how she would ever remember their names and what they did. Most new employees feel that way.

If you tour the workplace, pay close attention to where people are and what they're doing. Look at how people keep their work spaces and what they're wearing.

Observing what others do can help you fit in. Selena noticed that most of her co-workers were dressed neatly and conservatively. She was glad that she had worn a simple skirt and blouse.

Selena's office doesn't have a specific dress code, but some companies do. For example, some employers require men to wear shirts with collars and women to wear pantyhose and shoes, not sandals. Others may not allow employees to wear jeans or sneakers.

Companies may also have other policies that its workers are expected to know and follow. Some of the most common policies concern working hours, vacation, personal days, and sick leave.

Some companies have **employee manuals** that explain all of these rules. This written guide also may include information on fringe benefits, the structure of the company, and promotion procedures.

If your company has an employee manual, you should look through it when you start work. That way, you will become familiar with basic policies and rules.

You don't have to memorize the manual, but you should keep it handy. Then, when unexpected questions or situations come up, you will know where to look for the answers.

Instead of a manual, smaller companies may provide their employees with benefits brochures and a typed list of rules. Other employers may not provide much in writing.

If you need to ask questions about policies, follow the unwritten rules of the company **hierarchy**, or chain of command. In other words, don't go to your boss's boss until you've approached your boss first. And don't ever *assume* anything. It's much better to keep asking questions until you get the right answer than to guess and get it wrong.

What's a Form W-4?

In Section 6 you read that the federal government requires you to pay income taxes on the money you earn. The government uses this money to pay for the services it provides.

When you start a new job, you have to fill out a **withholding form**. This form determines how much money will be deducted from your salary for federal and other income taxes. It is called a **Form W-4**.

To fill out the Form W-4 correctly, you have to know how many **allowances** to declare. You can claim an allowance for each person, including yourself, who depends on your income for support. For each allowance you claim, you will have less tax deducted from your pay.

The Form W-4 comes with an attached worksheet, as shown on pages 70 and 71. In this example, Selena has claimed allowances for herself and her son, Leroy. She has also claimed an allowance as **head of household**. She can do this because she is a single parent who pays the household expenses.

The second page of the Form W-4 includes a special worksheet. People may need to use this if they **itemize** income tax deductions or if their earnings were above a certain level. These worksheets help you make sure that you aren't having too little or too much money deducted for taxes.

An employee who doesn't earn enough money to owe any federal tax may claim **exempt** status. You can find out if you qualify for exempt status by contacting the Internal Revenue Service.

199X Form W-4

Department of the Treasury Internal Revenue Service

Purpose. Complete Form W-4 so that your employer can withhold the correct amount of Federal income tax from your pay.

Exemption From Withholding. Read line 6 of the certificate below to see if you can claim exempt status. *If exempt, complete line 6; but do not complete lines 4 and 5.* No Federal income tax will be withheld from your pay. This exemption expires February 15, 199X.

Basic Instructions. Employees who are not exempt should complete the Personal Allowances Worksheet. Additional worksheets are provided on page 2 for employees to adjust their withholding allowances based on itemized deductions, adjustments to income, or two-earner/two-job situations. Complete all worksheets that apply to your situation. The worksheets will help you figure the number of withholding allowances you are

entitled to claim. However, you may claim fewer allowances than this.

Head of Household. Generally, you may claim head of household filing status on your tax return only if you are unmarried and pay more than 50% of the costs of keeping up a home for yourself and your dependent(s) or other qualifying individuals.

Nonwage Income. If you have a large amount of nonwage income, such as interest or dividends, you should consider making estimated tax payments using Form 1040-ES. Otherwise, you may find that you owe additional tax at the end of the year.

Two-Earner/Two-Jobs. If you have a working spouse or more than one job, figure the total number of allowances you are entitled to claim on all jobs using worksheets from only one Form

W-4. This total should be divided among all jobs. Your withholding will usually be most accurate when all allowances are claimed on the W-4 filed for the highest paying job and zero allowances are claimed for the others.

Advance Earned Income Credit. If you are eligible for this credit, you can receive it added to your paycheck throughout the year. For details, obtain Form W-5 from your employer.

Check Your Withholding. After your W-4 takes effect, you can use **Publication 919**, Is My Withholding Correct for 199X?, to see how the dollar amount you are having withheld compares to your estimated total annual tax. Call 1-800-424-3676 (in Hawaii and Alaska, check your local telephone directory) to order this publication. Check your local telephone directory for the IRS assistance number if you need further help.

Personal Allowances Worksheet

A   Enter "1" for **yourself** if no one else can claim you as a dependent . . . . **A**   1

B   Enter "1" if:
- **1.** You are single and have only one job; or
- **2.** You are married, have only one job, and your spouse does not work; or
- **3.** Your wages from a second job or your spouse's wages (or the total of both) are $2,500 or less.

    } . . . . . . **B**   1

C   Enter "1" for your **spouse.** But, you may choose to enter "0" if you are married and have either a working spouse or more than one job (this may help you avoid having too little tax withheld) . . . . **C**

D   Enter number of **dependents** (other than your spouse or yourself) whom you will claim on your tax return . . . . . **D**   1

E   Enter "1" if you will file as a **head of household** on your tax return (see conditions under "Head of Household," above) . . **E**   1

F   Enter "1" if you have at least $1,500 of **child or dependent care expenses** for which you plan to claim a credit . . . . **F**

G   Add lines A through F and enter total here . . . . ▶ **G**   4

For accuracy, do all worksheets that apply.
- If you plan to **itemize or claim adjustments to income** and want to reduce your withholding, turn to the Deductions and Adjustments Worksheet on page 2.
- If you are **single** and have **more than one job** and your combined earnings from all jobs exceed $25,000 OR if you are **married** and have a **working spouse or more than one job,** and the combined earnings from all jobs exceed $44,000, then turn to the Two-Earner/Two-Job Worksheet on page 2 if you want to avoid having too little tax withheld.
- If **neither** of the above situations applies to you, **stop here** and enter the number from line G on line 4 of Form W-4 below.

-------------- **Cut here and give the certificate to your employer. Keep the top portion for your records.** --------------

Form **W-4** Department of the Treasury Internal Revenue Service	**Employee's Withholding Allowance Certificate** ▶ For Privacy Act and Paperwork Reduction Act Notice, see reverse.		OMB No. 1545-0010 **199X**

1 Type or print your first name and middle initial   Last name   **2** Your social security number

   Selena   Price   078-41-4637

Home address (number and street or rural route)

   93 Willis Rd.

3 Marital status

☑ Single   ☐ Married

☐ Married, but withhold at higher Single rate.

Note: *If married, but legally separated, or spouse is a nonresident alien, check the Single box.*

City or town, state, and ZIP code

   Springfield , IL   62700

4 Total number of allowances you are claiming (from line G above or from the Worksheets on back if they apply) . . . **4**   4

5 Additional amount, if any, you want deducted from each pay . . . . **5** $

6 I claim exemption from withholding and I certify that I meet **ALL** of the following conditions for exemption:
- Last year I had a right to a refund of **ALL** Federal income tax withheld because I had **NO** tax liability; **AND**
- This year I expect a refund of **ALL** Federal income tax withheld because I expect to have **NO** tax liability; **AND**
- This year if my income exceeds $500 and includes nonwage income, another person cannot claim me as a dependent.

If you meet all of the above conditions, enter the year effective and "EXEMPT" here . . . . . ▶ **6**   19

7 Are you a full-time student? (**Note:** *Full-time students are not automatically exempt.*) . . . . **7** ☐ Yes   ☐ No

Under penalties of perjury, I certify that I am entitled to the number of withholding allowances claimed on this certificate or entitled to claim exempt status.

Employee's signature ▶   *Selena Price*   Date ▶   March 29 , 19 9X

8 Employer's name and address (**Employer:** Complete 8 and 10 **only if sending to IRS**)   **9** Office code (optional)   **10** Employer identification number

Deductions and Adjustments Worksheet

Note: *Use this worksheet only if you plan to itemize deductions or claim adjustments to income on your* 199X *tax return.*

1   Enter an estimate of your 199X itemized deductions. These include: qualifying home mortgage interest, 10% of personal interest, charitable contributions, state and local taxes (but not sales taxes), medical expenses in excess of 7.5% of your income, and miscellaneous deductions (most miscellaneous deductions are now deductible only in excess of 2% of your income) . . . . **1** $ _____

2   Enter: $\left\{\begin{array}{l}\text{\$5,450 if married filing jointly or qualifying widow(er)}\\\text{\$4,750 if head of household}\\\text{\$3,250 if single}\\\text{\$2,725 if married filing separately}\end{array}\right\}$ . . . . **2** $ _____

3   **Subtract** line 2 from line 1. If line 2 is greater than line 1, enter zero . . . . **3** $ _____

4   Enter an estimate of your 199X adjustments to income. These include alimony paid and deductible IRA contributions . **4** $ _____

5   **Add** lines 3 and 4 and enter the total . . . . **5** $ _____

6   Enter an estimate of your 199X nonwage income (such as dividends or interest income) . . . . **6** $ _____

7   **Subtract** line 6 from line 5. Enter the result, but not less than zero . . . . **7** $ _____

8   **Divide** the amount on line 7 by $2,000 and enter the result here. Drop any fraction . . . . . . **8** _____

9   Enter the number from Personal Allowances Worksheet, line G, on page 1 . . . . **9** _____

10   **Add** lines 8 and 9 and enter the total here. If you plan to use the Two-Earner/Two-Job Worksheet, also enter the total on line 1, below. Otherwise, **stop here** and enter this total on Form W-4, line 4 on page 1 . . . . **10** _____

Two-Earner/Two-Job Worksheet

Note: *Use this worksheet only if the instructions at line G on page 1 direct you here.*

1   Enter the number from line G on page 1 (or from line 10 above if you used the Deductions and Adjustments Worksheet) . **1** _____

2   Find the number in **Table 1** below that applies to the **LOWEST** paying job and enter it here . . . . . . **2** _____

3   If line 1 is **GREATER THAN OR EQUAL TO** line 2, subtract line 2 from line 1. Enter the result here (if zero, enter "0") and on Form W-4, line 4, on page 1. **DO NOT** use the rest of this worksheet . . . . **3** _____

Note: *If line 1 is **LESS THAN** line 2, enter "0" on Form W-4, line 4, on page 1. Complete lines 4–9 to calculate the additional dollar withholding necessary to avoid a year-end tax bill.*

4   Enter the number from line 2 of this worksheet . . . . **4** _____

5   Enter the number from line 1 of this worksheet . . . . **5** _____

6   **Subtract** line 5 from line 4 . . . . **6** _____

7   Find the amount in **Table 2** below that applies to the **HIGHEST** paying job and enter it here . . . . . . **7** $ _____

8   **Multiply** line 7 by line 6 and enter the result here. This is the additional annual withholding amount needed **8** $ _____

9   Divide line 8 by the number of pay periods each year. (For example, divide by 26 if you are paid every other week.) Enter the result here and on Form W-4, line 5, page 1. This is the additional amount to be withheld from each paycheck . . **9** $ _____

Table 1: Two-Earner/Two-Job Worksheet

Married Filing Jointly		All Others	
If wages from **LOWEST** paying job are—	Enter on line 2 above	If wages from **LOWEST** paying job are—	Enter on line 2 above
0 - $4,000	0	0 - $4,000	0
4,001 - 8,000	1	4,001 - 8,000	1
8,001 - 19,000	2	8,001 - 14,000	2
19,001 - 23,000	3	14,001 - 16,000	3
23,001 - 25,000	4	16,001 - 21,000	4
25,001 - 27,000	5	21,001 and over	5
27,001 - 29,000	6		
29,001 - 35,000	7		
35,001 - 41,000	8		
41,001 - 46,000	9		
46,001 and over	10		

Table 2: Two-Earner/Two-Job Worksheet

Married Filing Jointly		All Others	
If wages from **HIGHEST** paying job are—	Enter on line 7 above	If wages from **HIGHEST** paying job are—	Enter on line 7 above
0 - $44,000	$310	0 - $25,000	$310
44,001 - 90,000	570	25,001 - 52,000	570
90,001 and over	680	52,001 and over	680

Privacy Act and Paperwork Reduction Act Notice.—We ask for this information to carry out the Internal Revenue laws of the United States. We may give the information to the Department of Justice for civil or criminal litigation and to cities, states, and the District of Columbia for use in administering their tax laws. You are required to give this information to your employer.

The time needed to complete this form will vary depending on individual circumstances. The estimated average time is: **Recordkeeping** 46 min., **Learning about the law or the form** 10 min., **Preparing the form** 70 min. If you have comments concerning the accuracy of these time estimates or suggestions for making this form more simple, we would be happy to hear from you. You can write to the **Internal Revenue Service,** Washington, DC 20224, Attn: IRS Reports Clearance Officer, T:FP; or the **Office of Management and Budget,** Paperwork Reduction Project (1545-0010), Washington, DC 20503.

✩ U.S. Government Printing Office:1989-245-066

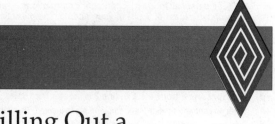

Filling Out a Form W-4

You have just started a new job. Your employer has handed you a Form W-4 to fill out.

Complete the form on page 73. Assume that you don't itemize deductions and you don't have exempt status.

How to Use Time Cards and Timesheets

If you work a full day, you should be paid for a full day. By filling in a time card or a timesheet each day, you can keep track of the hours and days you work. And then you and your employer will know how much you should be paid.

Time cards are used in factories and in many other workplaces that pay by the hour. Every day that you work, you fill in the time card with the date, the time you started work (in the *In* column), and the time you stopped work (in the *Out* column).

At the end of the week or pay period, you figure out how many hours you worked each day (in the *Hours* column). Then you add up those hours to get the number of hours worked. If you are paid by the hour, this figure will be used to compute your gross pay.

In some workplaces, time clocks are used to print the time of day when employees arrive and leave. Employees do this by inserting the time card into the time clock.

In Selena's office, timesheets are used instead of time cards. Timesheets are often used in jobs where workers are paid a weekly salary. In her job, Selena is expected to report on time each day and work 35 hours a week.

She is paid for an hour lunch each day she works. Her paycheck won't go up or down if she works an hour more or less each week.

Filling Out a Timesheet

The timesheet below has been partially filled out. Complete Selena Price's timesheet based on the following information:

♦ She came to work at 8:30 A.M. on Tuesday and left at 5:30 P.M.

♦ She was sick on Wednesday.

♦ She came to work at 9:30 A.M. on Thursday and stayed until 6:00 P.M.

♦ She came to work at 8:30 A.M. on Friday and left at noon to attend a work-related training class until 5:30 P.M.

EMPLOYEE TIMESHEET					
Department: 242					
Week of: Oct. 15 to Oct. 19					

Employee	**Mon.**	**Tues.**	**Wed.**	**Thurs.**	**Fri.**
Brenda Jones	IN 9:00	8:55	–	–	–
	OUT 5:10	4:55	–	–	–
Yoki Kimbo	IN 8:50	9:00	–	–	–
	OUT 5:00	5:15	–	–	–
Ralph Mendoza	IN 9:15	8:00	–	–	–
	OUT 6:00	5:00	–	–	–
Selena Price	IN 9:00				
	OUT 5:00				
	IN				
	OUT				
	IN				
	OUT				

199X Form W-4

Department of the Treasury
Internal Revenue Service

Purpose. Complete Form W-4 so that your employer can withhold the correct amount of Federal income tax from your pay.

Exemption From Withholding. Read line 6 of the certificate below to see if you can claim exempt status. *If exempt, complete line 6; but do not complete lines 4 and 5.* No Federal income tax will be withheld from your pay. This exemption expires February 15, 199X.

Basic Instructions. Employees who are not exempt should complete the Personal Allowances Worksheet. Additional worksheets are provided on page 2 for employees to adjust their withholding allowances based on itemized deductions, adjustments to income, or two-earner/two-job situations. Complete all worksheets that apply to your situation. The worksheets will help you figure the number of withholding allowances you are

entitled to claim. However, you may claim fewer allowances than this.

Head of Household. Generally, you may claim head of household filing status on your tax return only if you are unmarried and pay more than 50% of the costs of keeping up a home for yourself and your dependent(s) or other qualifying individuals.

Nonwage Income. If you have a large amount of nonwage income, such as interest or dividends, you should consider making estimated tax payments using Form 1040-ES. Otherwise, you may find that you owe additional tax at the end of the year.

Two-Earner/Two-Jobs. If you have a working spouse or more than one job, figure the total number of allowances you are entitled to claim on all jobs using worksheets from only one Form

W-4. This total should be divided among all jobs. Your withholding will usually be most accurate when all allowances are claimed on the W-4 filed for the highest paying job and zero allowances are claimed for the others.

Advance Earned Income Credit. If you are eligible for this credit, you can receive it added to your paycheck throughout the year. For details, obtain Form W-5 from your employer.

Check Your Withholding. After your W-4 takes effect, you can use **Publication 919**, Is My Withholding Correct for 199X?, to see how the dollar amount you are having withheld compares to your estimated total annual tax. Call 1-800-424-3676 (in Hawaii and Alaska, check your local telephone directory) to order this publication. Check your local telephone directory for the IRS assistance number if you need further help.

Personal Allowances Worksheet

A Enter "1" for **yourself** if no one else can claim you as a dependent . . . . **A** _____

B Enter "1" if:
  1. You are single and have only one job; or
  2. You are married, have only one job, and your spouse does not work; or
  3. Your wages from a second job or your spouse's wages (or the total of both) are $2,500 or less. **B** _____

C Enter "1" for your **spouse.** But, you may choose to enter "0" if you are married and have either a working spouse or more than one job (this may help you avoid having too little tax withheld) . . . . **C** _____

D Enter number of **dependents** (other than your spouse or yourself) whom you will claim on your tax return . . . . **D** _____

E Enter "1" if you will file as a **head of household** on your tax return (see conditions under "Head of Household," above) . . **E** _____

F Enter "1" if you have at least $1,500 of **child or dependent care expenses** for which you plan to claim a credit . . . . **F** _____

G Add lines A through F and enter total here . . . . ▶ **G** _____

For accuracy, do all worksheets that apply.
- If you plan to **itemize or claim adjustments to income** and want to reduce your withholding, turn to the Deductions and Adjustments Worksheet on page 2.
- If you are **single** and have **more than one job** and your combined earnings from all jobs exceed $25,000 OR if you are **married** and have a **working spouse or more than one job,** and the combined earnings from all jobs exceed $44,000, then turn to the Two-Earner/Two-Job Worksheet on page 2 if you want to avoid having too little tax withheld.
- If **neither** of the above situations applies to you, **stop here** and enter the number from line G on line 4 of Form W-4 below.

------------------ Cut here and give the certificate to your employer. Keep the top portion for your records. ------------------

| Form **W-4** Department of the Treasury Internal Revenue Service | **Employee's Withholding Allowance Certificate** ▶ **For Privacy Act and Paperwork Reduction Act Notice, see reverse.** | OMB No. 1545-0010 **199X** |

| **1** Type or print your first name and middle initial | Last name | **2** Your social security number |

| Home address (number and street or rural route) | **3** Marital status | ☐ Single ☐ Married ☐ Married, but withhold at higher Single rate. **Note:** *If married, but legally separated, or spouse is a nonresident alien, check the Single box.* |
| City or town, state, and ZIP code | | |

4 Total number of allowances you are claiming (from line G above or from the Worksheets on back if they apply) . . . **4** ____

5 Additional amount, if any, you want deducted from each pay . . . . **5** $____

6 I claim exemption from withholding and I certify that I meet **ALL** of the following conditions for exemption:
- Last year I had a right to a refund of **ALL** Federal income tax withheld because I had **NO** tax liability; **AND**
- This year I expect a refund of **ALL** Federal income tax withheld because I expect to have **NO** tax liability; **AND**
- This year if my income exceeds $500 and includes nonwage income, another person cannot claim me as a dependent.

If you meet all of the above conditions, enter the year effective and "EXEMPT" here . . . . . ▶ | **6** | 19

7 Are you a full-time student? (**Note:** *Full-time students are not automatically exempt.*) . . . . **7** ☐ Yes ☐ No

Under penalties of perjury, I certify that I am entitled to the number of withholding allowances claimed on this certificate or entitled to claim exempt status.

Employee's signature ▶ _____ Date ▶ _____ , 19

| **8** Employer's name and address (**Employer:** Complete 8 and 10 **only if sending to IRS**) | **9** Office code (optional) | **10** Employer identification number |

Understanding Insurance Forms

Many workers consider health insurance their most valuable fringe benefit. Health care and insurance costs have risen greatly over the last 10 years. A company may pay $2,000 or more a year for a family's health coverage.

About 9 out of 10 companies provide health insurance for their full-time employees. This saves workers money and contributes to their families' peace of mind. When you look for a job, keep in mind that comparing the different types of insurance offered and their cost to you may be almost as important as comparing salaries.

Companies also benefit from providing health coverage to employees. Workers are more likely to be more satisfied with their jobs if they receive adequate benefits, and satisfied workers are more reliable and productive.

Selena was very concerned about medical insurance since she is a single parent. She found out that for her, health coverage is provided free of charge by the company she works for. For a small fee, Selena could arrange to have Leroy, her dependent, covered, too.

In order to get health benefits, new workers usually must fill out insurance enrollment forms. On her first day, Selena went to the personnel department to fill out her enrollment form. On the form, she had to fill in details about her own health history as well as her son's.

When you fill out an insurance enrollment form, it is important to take your time and answer every question completely and accurately. Making a mistake or leaving out information might create problems later on. These forms can be very complicated to fill out. You might want to ask an employee in the personnel or benefits department to go over the form with you step by step.

Filling Out an Enrollment Card

You have just started a new job. You need to fill out the enrollment card on page 75. When you do so, follow these instructions:

♦ Check off *New Enrollment*.
♦ Enter your name, address, birth date, and Social Security number.
♦ Under *Sex*, check "male" or "female."
♦ Leave *Earnings* blank.
♦ Under *Occupation*, enter the job you now have, or one you plan to apply for.
♦ If your spouse or children would be covered, check off "Yes" for the question, *Do you wish dep. benefits?*
♦ If you check "Yes" to dependent benefits, enter the names, relationships, and birth dates of your dependents.
♦ Check "Yes" or "No" for supplemental benefits.

Comparing Health Insurance

Many companies offer employees a choice between **traditional health care insurance** and a **Health Maintenance Organization (HMO)**. Let's take a close look at each one.

Traditional Health Care Insurance

This coverage protects people from major medical expenses and loss of income due to health-related problems. The company you work for could pay for the entire plan. Or it might require workers to pay part of the cost. This is called a **co-pay** plan.

Benefits don't begin until you pay a certain part of the cost of your own medical care. The amount you must pay is called the **deductible**.

Enrollment Card

```
1. PLEASE TYPE OR PRINT CLEARLY                                    ENROLLMENT CARD
2. CARD MUST BE DATED AND SIGNED
```

| NOVA | ☐ New Enrollment ☐ Beneficiary Change | Date Employed Mo. Day Year | Account No. |
| | ☐ Reinstatement ☐ Change of Status | | |

| Last Name | First Name | M.I. | Sex ☐ M ☐ F | Social Security No. | Date of Birth Mo. Day Year |

| Address | Earnings | Occupation |

| Do you wish dep. benefits? Medical ☐ Yes ☐ No Dental ☐ Yes ☐ No | Do you want supplemental Benefits? ☐ Yes ☐ No | ☐ "In lieu of CG Medical Coverage, I am electing participation in _____ HMO. I am aware that should I later transfer to the CG Medical Plan limitations and exclusions may apply." |

Effective Date	List Your Eligible Dependents			Relationship			Date of Birth		
	Last Name (if different)	First Name	M.I.	Spouse	Son	Daughter	Mo.	Day	Year
Life									
AD&D									
DI/LTD	Name of Employer				Div.-Class-Location				
Medical	Beneficiary and relationship (First Name, Middle Initial, Last Name)								
Dental	Address of Beneficiary if not related to employee				Spouse's employer				

| Date | Signature |

For example, if you have a $100 deductible plan, you would pay the first $100 of your medical bills. The insurance company would pay the rest or a large percentage of it.

In these plans, people may have to pay their own bills and file claim forms with the insurance company to get money back. Most basic plans include the following:

♦ **Hospital and surgical insurance.** This pays for all or part of hospital bills and surgeons' fees as well as expenses from hospital stays.

♦ **Medical expense insurance.** This pays for doctors' fees for office visits and routine services.

♦ **Outpatient insurance.** This pays for medical treatment without a hospital stay.

♦ **Major medical insurance.** This pays for some other types of expenses.

Health Maintenance Organization (HMO)

HMOs operate differently than traditional health care insurance does. An HMO is a group or **association** of doctors who have organized to provide low-cost health care.

If you choose an HMO, first you must see the doctors who belong to the organization. You must also choose from a list of member hospitals, when possible. You can see any other doctor as long as you get a **referral** from your primary care physician.

Depending on the plan and your company's policy, you may have to pay part of the cost of the HMO. Although there may be a co-payment provision, or specific condition, in an HMO, there is no deductible. You pay either nothing or a very small fee for medical services. You can also get services such as routine checkups for free.

If your company offers both types of plans, pick the one that best meets your needs. For example, if you have a doctor you want to keep seeing, you may choose traditional health insurance. If you want to save money on health care, you may choose an HMO.

Your First Paycheck

It's a great feeling to receive your first paycheck. But some people are surprised when they read the amount. This can happen if you are expecting to receive your gross pay and have forgotten about the deductions.

Look at the copy of Selena's paycheck. It includes the date, her name, and the name and address of the company and its bank.

Along with a paycheck comes a form called a **paystub**. It shows how your gross pay is broken down into all its separate deductions.

Look at the copy of Selena's paystub below. As you can see, she earned $420 in gross pay. And she paid $102 for deductions. The deductions include her medical insurance, social security tax, federal income tax, disabil-

---

ABC BUSINESS MACHINES
1260 WALL STREET EAST
PARKHURST, IL 62702

FIRST NATIONAL BANK
Downtown Office
Riverside, IL 62704

7969

| DATE | Oct. 26, 199X |
| AMOUNT | $318.00 |

PAY   Three Hundred Eighteen and 00/100 Dollars

TO THE
ORDER
OF

SELENA PRICE
93 WILLIS ROAD
SPRINGFIELD, IL 62700

J. J. Jenkins

⑈007968⑈ ⑆000067894⑆ 12345678⑈

ABC BUSINESS MACHINES

7969

PAY PERIOD ENDING: 10-19-199X

EMPLOYEE NO: 13-1824180   EMPLOYEE NAME: SELENA PRICE   SOCIAL SECURITY NUMBER: 078-41-4637

DESCRIPTION	CURRENT	YEAR-TO-DATE	DESCRIPTION	CURRENT	YEAR-TO-DATE
REGULAR	420.00	17,640.00	FICA	32.13	1,349.46
OVERTIME	.00	.00	FED. TAX	49.87	2,094.54
			DIS./UN.	5.90	247.80
			STATE TAX	10.10	424.20
			MED. INS.	4.00	168.00
TOTALS:	420.00	17,640.00		102.00	4,284.00
			NET PAY: 318.00		

ity and unemployment insurance, and state income tax. Her net, or take-home, pay is $318.00.

Compare the date on Selena's check with the date on the paystub next to the category "Pay Period Ending." As you can see, the paycheck is dated one full week after the end of the pay period. This means that *this* week's check is for *last* week's work.

Many companies pay on this schedule. It takes time for them to total each week's hours and write out the checks. For this reason, new employees may have to wait an extra week for their first paycheck. You should ask when you will be receiving your first paycheck.

When you get your paycheck, you may have questions about the deductions. If you do, ask someone in the payroll or personnel department. The amounts taken out for taxes are based primarily on the information you provided on the Form W-4.

It's a good idea to look over your paystub every payday. Keep a record of the amounts that should be deducted. If these figures change, contact the payroll department to find out why.

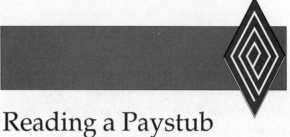

Reading a Paystub

Read the paystub below. Then compare the figures on the paystub to the information below.

Employee: Mauricio Rojas
Marital status: Single
Number of dependents: 0
Weekly contribution to savings plan: $10.00
Company-wide medical insurance costs: $9.75/family; $6.25/individual

Can you find any errors in the paystub? If so, what are they? _____

_____

_____

_____

_____

4531

EMPLOYEE NO: 2198   EMPLOYEE NAME: MAURICIO ROJAS   PAY PERIOD ENDING: 3-12-9X

DESCRIPTION	CURRENT	YEAR-TO-DATE	DESCRIPTION	CURRENT	YEAR-TO-DATE
REGULAR	390.00	390.00	FICA	29.84	29.84
			FED. TAX	45.16	45.16
			DIS./UN.	4.20	4.20
			STATE TAX	7.80	7.80
			MED. INS.	9.75	9.75
			SAVINGS	.00	.00
TOTALS:	390.00	390.00		96.75	96.75
			NET PAY: 293.25		

What's a Form W-2?

When you have a job, your employer will give you a **Form W-2** each January. This is a wage and tax statement. It shows how much money you earned during the past year. It also shows how much money was deducted for taxes. Below is an example of Selena's Form W-2. You will get at least three copies of your W-2 statement. One is for you to keep. One goes to the federal government and one to the state government when you file your **income tax return**.

A tax return is a form used to state your income and on which you figure out the total amount of tax you should have paid for the past year. You must file an income tax return by April 15 each year if your earnings were above a certain level.

When you send in your income tax return, you must include a copy of your W-2 statement from each employer you have worked for. If the amount of taxes deducted from your pay was not enough, then you must send a check to the government along with your return. If too much money was deducted, you will get a refund.

Points to Remember

In this section you learned about adjusting to your first days on a new job. To make that adjustment easier, be sure to:

♦ learn as much as possible about your job responsibilities and about the company
♦ refer to the employee manual for company rules and policies
♦ fill out the Form W-4 carefully
♦ use time cards and timesheets correctly
♦ understand how to fill out insurance forms
♦ know what to expect in your first paycheck

SELENA'S FORM W-2

1 Control number 094863 C2L	22222	For Paperwork Reduction Act Notice, see back of Copy D. OMB No. 1545-0008	For Official Use Only ▶	
2 Employer's name, address, and ZIP code		3 Employer's identification number 13-1824180		4 Employer's state I.D. number 131824180
ABC Business Machines 1260 Wall St. East Parkhurst, IL 62702		5 Statutory employee ☐ Deceased ☐ Pension plan ☐ Legal rep. ☐	942 emp. ☐ Subtotal ☐ Deferred compensation ☐ Void ☐	
		6 Allocated tips	7 Advance EIC payment	
8 Employee's social security number 078-41-4637	9 Federal income tax withheld 2,080.00	10 Wages, tips, other compensation 21,840.00	11 Social security tax withheld 1,248.00	
12 Employee's name (first, middle, last) Selena Price		13 Social security wages 21,840.00	14 Social security tips	
		16 (See Instr. for Forms W-2/W-2P)	16a Fringe benefits incl. in Box 10	
93 Willis Rd. Springfield, IL 62700		17 State income tax 416.00	18 State wages, tips, etc. 21,840.00	19 Name of state IL
15 Employee's address and ZIP code		20 Local income tax 135.20	21 Local wages, tips, etc. 21,840.00	22 Name of locality Parkhurst

Form **W-2 Wage and Tax Statement 199X**
95-2830662   APR. I.R.S.

Copy A For Social Security Administration   Dept. of the Treasury—IRS

When Selena files her income tax return with the federal government, she will send along a copy of her Form W-2.

Word-Wise

Fill in the blanks below to complete the sentences. The answers are key terms introduced in this section.

1. You can claim an _____ for each person who depends on your income.

2. The _____ is the chain of command in a company.

3. If you're a single parent who pays the expenses for your family, then you can claim _____ _____ _____ status on your income tax return.

4. When you start a new job, whether or not you like it, expect to go through an _____ _____.

5. Your responsibilities and everyday duties at work are written in a _____ _____.

6. Many health insurance plans require people to pay a _____ before the benefits begin.

7. You should fill out a _____ for the government when you start a new job.

Putting It to Work

You are in charge of showing a new employee the basics on his first day. Name five things you would do to make his adjustment easier.

1. _____
2. _____
3. _____
4. _____
5. _____

You Be the Judge

You have just started a new job. The company offers its employees a traditional health insurance plan and an HMO plan. You have to make the decision today. Which would you choose? _____
_____

Explain why. _____
_____
_____
_____
_____
_____

Getting the Facts

You have started a new job. You have a few questions concerning deductions, exemptions, and allowances. What government agency would you contact? _____
_____

Now find the address and telephone number of that agency.

Address: _____

Phone number: _____

Where did you find that information?
_____
_____

Now call to find out how much money you can earn before you have to pay taxes.
_____

SECTION 8

A BALANCING ACT

As Anita put on her coat, she looked over at Lydell. He was getting ready to leave work, too. Lydell was silent and unhappy like he'd been for days.

"What's wrong?" Anita asked.

"Nothing," Lydell replied.

"You can talk to me," Anita said. "Let me buy you a cup of coffee."

"OK," Lydell said, "but I can't stay long. I have to get home."

As she sipped her coffee, Anita said, "What's the matter? You haven't been yourself lately."

"I've been having problems with Jay."

"Is he sick?" Anita asked.

"No, *he's* not sick," Lydell answered. "But his regular babysitter is. The new babysitter is terrible. She shows up late. I don't think she takes very good care of Jay. But I can't find anybody else to watch him."

"So that's why you've been late this week," Anita said.

"Yes," Lydell said. "And Mr. Ross yelled at me about it."

"Did you tell him why you were late?" Anita asked.

"No," Lydell said.

"If you explained it to him, I know he would understand," Anita said.

"All right," Lydell said. "I'll talk to him tomorrow."

"Maybe you could talk to a few other people, too," Anita said. "You've been snapping at your friends."

"Boy, I hadn't realized I was giving everyone such a hard time," Lydell said.

"We want to help," Anita said.

"But how can you?" Lydell asked.

"We can give you moral support," Anita said. "And we may know a babysitter who can help you out."

"Do you think so?" Lydell asked.

"It's worth a try, isn't it?" Anita asked.

"Yes, it is," Lydell said as he smiled.

Juggling work and personal demands is a part of many people's lives.
Do you ever feel as though you're juggling too many things?

Balancing Work and Family

Working parents like Lydell have to be jugglers. They have to juggle the demands of work and family. Many parents are afraid that if they let one thing slip, everything will fall apart. Like Lydell, they sometimes find the pressure hard to take.

Every person plays many **roles** in life, and pressure often results from juggling these roles. You play a role as someone's daughter or son. Perhaps you play another role as a wife or husband. Another role you may play is as a parent. You may also be a friend, a homemaker, and an employee. Each of these roles has its own set of demands.

Many Roles, Many Demands

Let's look at two areas of life—work and personal life. Depending on your roles, some of the basic demands you might face in each area are listed below.

Work demands include:
♦ coming in on time
♦ working the required number of hours
♦ being reliable and hardworking
♦ doing each task correctly
♦ following company rules and policies
♦ getting along with your supervisor and employer
♦ working well with co-workers
♦ traveling or working overtime if needed
♦ growing with the job so you can take on more responsibilities

Personal demands may include:
♦ meeting your family's and your own needs for food, clothing, and a clean, safe home
♦ taking care of your children
♦ spending time with your spouse
♦ maintaining your health
♦ caring for sick family members
♦ working on educational or career goals
♦ taking part in community or religious activities

Many mothers don't have another adult to help them meet the demands of going to work and caring for children.

♦ spending time with friends
♦ using free time for hobbies or relaxation

Think about the list of demands you just read. They seem easy enough to meet, don't they? But what does it really take to meet all of them?

For instance, consider the demand of providing food, clothing, and a clean, safe home for your family. After a full day at work, a working parent like Lydell might spend several hours cooking, doing laundry, and straightening up the house.

Later, school-age children may need help with their homework. A grandparent may need a ride to the doctor. And you may have to attend a community meeting.

In some homes two adults share all of these tasks. But the number of single-parent households is growing. And it's usually the mother who has to juggle all the demands alone.

It's easy to see why working parents say there aren't enough hours in a day. And when things in one area of life don't go smoothly, meeting demands in other areas can seem even harder.

Managing Your Time

What can you, as a working parent or a busy person, do to make meeting demands easier? The answer is to manage your time more effectively. By planning the hours in your day, you can get more done in a limited amount of time.

Here are the basic steps in managing your time:

1. Make a list of personal goals.
2. Put goals in their order of importance. This is called **setting priorities.**
3. Study the way you use time now. Find ways to make improvements.
4. Make a list of the goals you can accomplish in the time you have.

5. Make a schedule for using your time so you can work to reach your goals.

Let's take a look at how better time management could work for Lydell. To start the process, he would think about what he wants to accomplish. His list includes **short-term goals.** Those are things that need to be done right away. Lydell's short-term goals include finding a new babysitter for his son, Jay, talking to his boss about the babysitter, and getting his car repaired.

Lydell will also have **long-term goals.** These will take more time to accomplish. Lydell's long-term goals include enrolling in a chef's course, moving to a nicer apartment, and taking Jay on a trip to visit his grandparents.

After Lydell lists these goals, he puts them in order, from most to least important. He decides that talking to his boss, Mr. Ross, might be the most important short-term goal. Talking to his boss would help Lydell protect his job and would also give Lydell greater peace of mind.

Lydell's most important long-term goal is taking a chef's course. This extra education would help Lydell get a promotion. The promotion would help him afford a nicer apartment and pay for the trip he wants to take.

Knowing his short-term goals helps Lydell schedule his time for the next few days. He plans to use one day's lunch hour to talk to Mr. Ross. The rest of the week, he will use his lunch hour to look for babysitters.

Lydell plans to ask a co-worker to pick him up for work while his car is being repaired. Getting help from others, as well as giving it, is an essential part of time management.

Before Lydell can make any plans for reaching long-term goals, he needs to look more closely at how he uses his time. For example, the chef's course would take several hours a week in class and at home. In order to make time to study, Lydell would have to cut down on the amount of time he watches TV.

To attend evening classes, Lydell could swap child care favors with his sister, Charlene. Then she could leave her daughter with Lydell and Jay on Sundays so she could use that time to pursue her own goals.

Putting Goals in Order

Like Lydell, you probably have goals that you want to reach. Some of your goals may be immediate, and others may be long range.

List some of your goals below. Include at least one goal from your work life and one goal from your personal life.

Next look at the lists of goals you made. Finally ask yourself which goals in each list are most important to you. Set your priorities now by numbering each short-term goal from 1 (most important) to 5 (least important). Write the number next to the goal. Do the same for each long-term goal.

Short-Term Goals:

_____ # _____

_____ # _____

_____ # _____

_____ # _____

_____ # _____

Long-Term Goals:

_____ # _____

_____ # _____

_____ # _____

_____ # _____

_____ # _____

Using Time Wisely

To reach your goals, you may have to cut out some activities that waste time. Lydell knew he would have to watch less TV if he wanted to have time to study and go to class.

How do you use your time? List three ways you waste time and the amount of time you spend on each per day or per week. Write how you could better use that time to reach one of your goals.

Time waster #1: _____

_____

Amount of time you spend: _____ per____

A better use of time: _____

_____

_____

Time waster #2: _____

_____

Amount of time you spend: _____ per____

A better use of time: _____

_____

_____

Time waster #3: _____

_____

Amount of time you spend: _____ per____

A better use of time: _____

_____

_____

Handling Child Care

Child care can be one of the most difficult demands for parents to handle. At one time or another, every working parent has prob-

lems like Lydell did. Parents who aren't sure whether their children are getting good care can't keep their minds on work. They are too busy worrying about their children. That's why it's so important to find a child care arrangement that you're happy and comfortable with.

If you were Lydell, you could begin your search for better child care arrangements by talking to co-workers who are parents. They might be able to recommend a convenient child care center that their children go to. Friends, relatives, and members of the clergy may also know reliable child care facilities or babysitters.

Lydell might also look through the newspaper for child care and babysitting ads. Or he could put an ad for a babysitter in a neighborhood paper.

Some communities have a **referral service**. If your community provides this service, you might be able to get a recommendation for a good child care center in your area. Or you might be able to get a listing of centers. You can find out more about this community service by looking under the headings "Child Care" or "Day Care" in your phone book.

When you look for child care, you will notice that there are three basic types of care available. They include:

♦ **Care in the child's home.** A child care provider lives in the child's home or comes there every morning and leaves at night.

♦ **Family child care.** The child is taken to the provider's home every day. In most cases, there are several other children there as well.

♦ **Child care center.** The child and a group of other children are cared for by a staff of adults. The center may be in a school, community building, church or synagogue, or office building.

Each type of child care arrangement has good and bad points. Care in the child's home is convenient, but it's usually expensive. Family child care costs less and allows children to **socialize**, or be with other children. But most family providers aren't trained teachers.

Child care centers are usually affordable and have a trained staff. In addition, centers must meet certain health, safety, and staffing requirements. But some centers are too crowded. And those that aren't crowded may be too expensive.

Some families decide that child care facilities are not right for them. Instead, they plan other ways to take care of their children while they work.

Lydell's sister, Charlene, works at home. She types contracts and other legal documents for a law firm. The company she works for bought her a computer to use at home. Charlene plans to keep working at home until her daughter starts first grade. Then Charlene will go back to working outside the home during the hours her daughter is in school.

Juan, a baker at Lydell's company, works the early shift, from 4 A.M. to noon. His wife, Gloria, goes to work at a hospital from 4 P.M. to midnight. This working arrangement lets them take turns caring for their three young children, so Juan and Gloria don't have to put the children in a child care center.

Comparing Child Care Arrangements

Before you choose a child care arrangement, you should examine it closely. When you visit a child care center or talk to a child care provider, ask some or all of the following questions.

♦ During what hours is care available?
♦ What does it cost?
♦ Are parents encouraged to drop in any time? (They should be.)
♦ Where is it located, and how easy is it to get there?
♦ Is it licensed?

♦ How many children are supervised by each adult? (The numbers that are acceptable vary from state to state. You should check your own state's regulations.)
♦ What is each provider's experience or training?
♦ Do you like the provider(s)?
♦ Does each provider enjoy being with children?
♦ Is there enough space for the number of children being cared for?
♦ Are there interesting things to do inside and outside?
♦ Is the indoor space safe and sanitary?
♦ Is it a cheerful place?
♦ Do the children seem happy?
♦ What happens if a child is sick?
♦ How are emergencies handled?
♦ How is misbehavior handled?
♦ How are mealtimes handled?

Child Care Help for Low-Income Families

Every year more parents need full-time child care for their children. But many parents can't afford to pay the high cost of full-time care.

There are government programs that can help. Some of these programs set up child care centers that charge very low rates. Other government programs may help by paying the cost of child care for parents who can't afford it.

Each state has different rules for helping low-income families. You can find out what help is available in your area by looking under the following headings in your local phone book:

♦ Day Care Council
♦ Department of Health and Human Services
♦ Economic Opportunity Commission
♦ Head Start Child Development Program Inc.
♦ Health and Welfare Council
♦ Child Development

If you call a government agency, ask if there are programs and if there are any openings. If the programs are available but they're full, find out if you can still fill out the forms and be put on a waiting list. That way when there is an opening, you will be notified.

Protecting Latchkey Children

Lydell was surprised to find out that some parents let their school-age children stay home alone for several hours a day. Child care experts disagree on whether or not this arrangement is good for **latchkey** children. But they all agree that there are some things parents can do to help protect children when they're on their own. These include:

♦ having children take a safety course at a local school, library, church, or YMCA
♦ sending away for information on safety from the county cooperative extension, child welfare agency, or utility company
♦ arranging for the child to call the parent or another responsible adult every day as soon as the child gets home from school
♦ making sure the child knows how to call the police, fire department, and emergency services, such as the 911 emergency number

If you're unhappy with your child being alone during the day, check to see if there are any after-school programs in your community. Many schools and community groups run free or low-cost after-school programs. To find out more, contact your local school district.

Budgeting Your Money

Another demand that can be difficult to deal with is handling money. If you never have any money left over a few days after you're paid, you will need to manage your money more effectively.

Like time management, you start to manage your money by setting short-term and long-term goals. Then you set priorities. The things you and your family *need* come first. The things you *want* come next. After that, you figure out how you have been using your money.

Based on all of that information, you make a plan that allows you to control spending and pay your necessary bills. This spending plan is called a **budget**.

Lydell needed a budget. He had to be sure that he could afford to pay for the child care he wanted. Luckily, the mailing he received from the county child care agency included a money management booklet with a budget worksheet. All Lydell had to do to figure out his budget was fill in the numbers.

On page 87 is a copy of the worksheet Lydell used to figure out how he was spending his money. Notice how the money is divided into the following categories:

♦ **Fixed expenses.** These are expenses that are paid every month, and they're usually the same amount. An example of a fixed expense would be your rent or your electricity bill.
♦ **Variable expenses.** These are expenses that you have occasionally. An estimate of what you usually spend for these kinds of expenses is used on the worksheet. An example of a variable expense would be money spent on clothing.
♦ **Spending money.** This is money you use for entertainment or day-to-day expenses, such as newspapers and coffee. Many people cannot pinpoint how they spend this money.

When Lydell added up the worksheet, he realized that he was spending an average of $5 more than he earned each month. That explained why he was always borrowing money from Charlene. Lydell decided to talk to his uncle about managing his money. Lydell's uncle had taken a lot of courses in personal finance.

Lydell knew he couldn't change most of his fixed and variable expenses, such as rent and medical costs. But his uncle showed Lydell that he could control his spending in small ways. Lydell decided to cut the amount of his pocket money in half. He also started walking to nearby places more often instead of driving.

These simple changes meant that Lydell wouldn't spend more than he made. But Lydell still had one major problem. He didn't have any money saved. Lydell's uncle told him that everyone who earns an income should save money regularly, even if it's only a small amount.

There are many reasons to save money. You may need it if there's an emergency, such as your spouse's becoming disabled. You can save for a child's education, a vacation, or a down payment on a car or house.

Lydell thought that the only people who saved money had much higher incomes than he did. He also thought that he could save only if he had money left over at the end of the month—and he never did.

Lydell learned that all people who earn an income should save some money. But, in order to do so, people need to make saving a priority. Lydell decided to have money automatically deducted from his paycheck at work and put into a savings plan. He planned to have $5 taken out each week at first. Later on, he would try to save more.

Like many people, Lydell had fallen into the overspending trap. In the past, he had used a credit card to pay for things he couldn't afford to buy with cash. Now he was stuck paying $110 a month toward his bills. Almost $20 of that payment was **interest**.

LYDELL'S SAMPLE BUDGET

Monthly Net Income	$1,495
Fixed Expenses	
Rent	$450
Car Payment	$150
Car Insurance	$90
Electricity	$30
Cooking Gas	$10
Telephone	$20
Credit Card Payments	$110
Gasoline	$30
Babysitter	$215
Food	$200
Savings	0
TOTAL	$1,305
Variable Expenses	
Household Items	$20
Clothing	$40
Medical Costs	$35
Auto Repair	$20
Charity	$10
Spending Money	
Entertainment	$30
Pocket Money	$40
TOTAL	$195

Interest is a fee that banks or other lending institutions charge people for borrowing money.

Once Lydell paid off his bills, he would change his budget to include less money for credit card purchases. He would only charge the amount he could pay off each month. That way, he wouldn't have to pay interest charges any more.

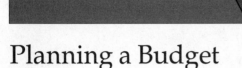

Planning a Budget

Suppose that you work and that your monthly net income is $1,145. You have the following expenses each month:

    Rent—$600
    Transportation—$85
    Medical Costs—$40
    Clothing—$50
    Electricity—$40
    Telephone—$30
    Food—$175

Use what you have learned about managing money to complete the budget below. Write in the monthly income figure. Then divide the seven figures you have been given between the categories of fixed expenses and variable expenses. Then add up the figures to get a total and answer the questions that follow.

Monthly Net Income $ _____

Fixed Expenses

_____ $ _____

_____ $ _____

_____ $ _____

_____ $ _____

_____ $ _____

Variable Expenses

_____ $ _____

_____ $ _____

Total $ _____

1. How much money is left over each month? _____

2. How would you use that money? _____

_____

_____

Moving

Many people have to move at one time or another. People move for many reasons. Some have to move for a new job. Others may have to move because their spouse is being transferred. Some move so they can live close to family or friends. Whatever the reason is, and whether you're moving across the country or across town, moving is very demanding.

There are so many details to handle, especially if you have a family. You might wonder where you'll live. Will you like your new job? Or will you be able to find a new job? How much will the move cost? Will your children adjust to the new school? And, will you be able to manage all these demands on top of what you already have to handle?

Moving may seem like an overwhelming task. But there are some ways to make it easier.

Before you move:
♦ Drop by the local office of a national moving or van rental company. (These companies are usually listed in the yellow pages of the phone book.) Ask for a moving guide to help you get organized.
♦ Contact a real estate office in the town you're moving to and ask them to send you a map of the area. The real estate office may also have booklets of facts about the community.
♦ Get the name and address of the town or city newspaper where you will be moving. Pay to have the newspaper sent to you by mail for a few weeks before you move. Read about houses and apartments, job openings, child care, and community events.

Then, as soon as you move:
♦ Get a copy of the yellow pages to find out about places to shop, things to do, and businesses where you could apply for a job.
♦ Arrange for a tour of your children's new school. Talk to the teachers and administra-

tors. Find out about after-school sports and clubs.

♦ Meet people by attending a local church, synagogue, or community organization.

And, throughout the whole process:

♦ Try to stick to routines. Routines are especially important during times of change.

♦ Talk to your children and spouse. Sharing your feelings can help put others at ease.

♦ Be patient if it takes time to adjust. Keep your cool and your sense of humor.

♦ Set aside time for packing and figuring out what to move.

Dealing with Personal and Family Illness

Illness can throw many people's lives off balance. When you're sick and can't report for work, call your supervisor as soon as you know you won't be able to go to work. If you're too sick to call, have another adult call work for you.

Don't report for work if you're sick. Doing so can cause problems. You may cause accidents on the job, or you may spread your illness. And if you're not feeling well, you won't work as effectively or efficiently as usual.

There is a limit to the number of sick days most employees are allowed. It's always a good idea to find out what your company's policy is *before* you need time off.

If you anticipate being out of work for a week or more, get a doctor's note explaining the illness or the injury. Employees who must miss a lot of time may receive disability pay for a limited time.

If you've been injured on the job, let your supervisor know as soon as it happens. You will probably have to fill out forms for your company and the insurance company. In this case, time off may be handled differently—so find out your company's policy by reading

A family member's illness usually places extra demands on a worker.

your employee manual.

If you have to take time off because your child or another relative is sick, let your supervisor know as soon as possible. This will probably be considered personal time. If you need extended personal time off, you may have to take a personal leave. Personal leaves are usually without pay.

Tell your supervisor if you will have to miss work for an extended period of time. That way, you won't be leaving the company or your department without help. Your supervisor may even arrange for someone else to handle your job until you can return.

Stress Management

The demands we've covered in this section are present in many workers' lives. And the continuous pressure of those demands adds up to **stress.** You probably know what stress feels like—sweaty palms, knotted stomach, rapid breathing, and pounding heart. But do you know where stress comes from?

Stress is the body's reaction to the demands of life. Stress is caused mainly by change. Many situations cause stress. Some situations can cause positive stress, such as when you're getting married or starting a new job. Some situations can cause negative stress, such as when you're dealing with a death in your family or having a fight with your spouse.

There's no way to take all the stress out of life. In some cases, stress can help you do your best. For example, stress causes the adrenaline to flow so that athletes can do their best in a competition. But too much stress can be harmful.

How can you keep the stress in your life to a minimum? First, you can try to be realistic about how many demands you can handle. Don't take on any more than you can manage. This is where managing your time can be of importance.

Second, be prepared for stress that can't be avoided. Realize that changes and problems happen in everybody's life. Remember how Lydell's babysitter got sick? That was bound to happen eventually. But it caused a lot of stress for him, because he wasn't prepared for it.

This time, Lydell chose a child care center with a staff of workers. He also arranged for a neighbor to watch Jay when the child was too sick to go to the center. And the next time, Lydell will talk to his friends and his supervisor as soon as things start to go wrong. Lydell has learned a lot about **coping**, or handling the stress.

How Much Stress Is Too Much?

How do you know whether you're under too much stress? Ask yourself

(continued)

the following questions to see if you are.
- Do I lose my temper over every little thing?
- Do I have trouble concentrating?
- Do I get tired very quickly?
- Do I have trouble relaxing or sleeping?
- Have I lost interest in people and activities that I used to enjoy?
- Do I worry constantly?
- Do I depend on alcohol or drugs to relax?
- Do I overeat, or have I lost my appetite?

If you answered yes to one or more of the questions above, then you may have too much stress in your life. Learning how to cope with that stress can help you minimize it. The following information will show you specific ways to cope.

Coping with Stress

What can you do to control the effects of stress? Here are some ways that people minimize the effects of stress. Rate how well you do each one by giving yourself a number from 0 (poor) to 5 (excellent). The higher your final score is, the better your coping skills are.

_____**Exercise.** This includes walking, swimming, dancing, and any other exercise you do a few times a week.

_____**Rest.** Try to get at least seven or eight hours of rest a night. If you have trouble sleeping, try to get more exercise. If that doesn't help, see your doctor.

_____**Communicate.** Talk to a trusted friend or relative about your feelings. If you have problems at work, discuss them with your supervisor or someone in the human resources department.

_____**Compromise.** You can't always have what you want. So, instead of fighting, **compromise** and find an alternative. Compromising is less stressful than fighting.

_____**Have fun.** Making time for hobbies and activities that you enjoy can help you relax.

_____**Get involved.** Find a worthy cause or an activity that gives you a lot of satisfaction—even if you can do it only for a short time each week or month.

_____**Improve your surroundings.** Make your environment at home and at work as peaceful as possible.

_____**Avoid drugs and alcohol.** Alcohol and drugs don't really relax you at all. They just leave you feeling depressed, and they create more stress.

Points to Remember

In this section, you learned that working people have to handle many different demands. Most working people have to do some of the following:

♦ balance work and family
♦ manage time
♦ set short-term and long-term goals
♦ find good child care
♦ manage money
♦ move to a new home
♦ deal with personal and family illness
♦ cope with stress

 C H E C K P O I N T

Word-Wise

Complete the paragraph below by writing in the correct word or words. The answers are key terms introduced in this section.

Each _____ you play in life has its own set of demands. You can make meeting those demands easier by managing your time. To do that, you need to _____ based on goals, both _____ and _____. You can also make meeting demands easier by making a spending plan called a _____ _____. If you do these things, you will be better able to _____ with

_____, the continuous pressure from demands.

Putting It to Work

You are the parent of a two-year-old child. You have just been offered a full-time job that you want to take. However, you must find a dependable child care arrangement for your child while you work.

Make a list of five important things you would look for in choosing child care.

1. _____
2. _____
3. _____
4. _____
5. _____

You Be the Judge

Your mother is sick and you have to take time off from work to care for her. What would you do?

_____

_____

_____

_____

Getting the Facts

You are going to start a new job and have to find a child care arrangement for your one-year-old daughter.

Using any of the sources mentioned in this chapter, find at least three arrangements in your area. Use the list of questions on page 85 to evaluate each arrangement. Then answer the questions below.

Arrangement #1: _____

_____

Where did you find out about this arrangement? _____

_____

_____

What are the good points? _____

_____

_____

What are the bad points? _____

_____

_____

Arrangement #2: _____

_____

Where did you find out about this arrangement? _____

_____

What are the good points? _____

_____

_____

What are the bad points? _____

_____

_____

Arrangement #3: _____

_____

Where did you find out about this arrangement? _____

_____

_____

What are the good points? _____

_____

_____

What are the bad points? _____

_____

_____

Which arrangement would you choose? ____

_____

Explain why. (If you wouldn't choose any of them, explain why not.) _____

_____

_____

_____

SECTION 9

PROTECTING YOUR RIGHTS

"Congratulations, Mel," Phil, a business lawyer, said. "Your incorporation papers were approved. You're now officially in the catering business."

"That's great!" Mel said, smiling. "Now I can start hiring."

"Sure," Phil said. "You can start as soon as you want to."

"Phil," Mel said. "I've never hired people before. What are the main legal things I need to know?"

"Well," Phil replied. "The first thing you need to keep in mind is your employee's rights."

"OK," Mel said. "I know something about that. For instance, I know that I can't discriminate against anyone because of race or sex. That's equal opportunity employment."

"Exactly," Phil said. "And if women who work for you get pregnant, you can't fire them."

"No, of course not," Mel said.

"Another important issue is safety," Phil said. "You have to provide safe working conditions for your employees. There are lots of laws about that."

"That makes sense," Mel said. "Is there anything else I should know?"

"Well, of course, you have to treat everyone fairly and equally," Phil replied. "And you know that there are

regulations about working hours, unions, and things like that."

"There are so many laws and rules," Mel said. "Do you have written information I could read over?"

"Here," Phil said, pulling some books and pamphlets out of his desk drawer. "All the information you need is in these. If you have any questions after you read them, give me a call."

"Thanks," Mel said, as he took the information. "I couldn't have done it without you."

Do You Know Your Rights?

Like Mel, few people know all of the rights that workers have on the job. Let's take a look at five specific federal laws that Mel read about in the books and pamphlets that Phil gave him.

♦ The Civil Rights Act of 1964 says that employers can't make hiring decisions based on gender, race, religion, nationality, or handicaps.

♦ The Equal Pay Act of 1963 says that employers must pay the same wages to male and female employees who do the same work.

♦ The Age Discrimination Employment Act of 1967 protects workers, especially those between the ages of 40 and 70, against age discrimination.

♦ The Pregnancy Discrimination Act of 1968 says that pregnant workers cannot be forced to leave a job early because of their pregnancy unless their job involves a safety or health hazard.

♦ The National Labor Relations Act of 1935 forbids discrimination against employees because of union activity.

What Form of Discrimination Is It?

The five situations that follow are ones that an individual could encounter on a job. Each situation involves a federal law that has been broken.

Read each situation, and on the line that follows, write what form of discrimination has occurred. Refer to the laws Mel read about if you need help.

1. Paul's boss told him he would lose his job if he kept talking with his co-workers about forming a union. _____

_____

2. When Lori was six months pregnant, her manager told her she had to go on maternity leave, without pay. _____

_____

3. An employer says he won't hire Carla because he thinks men are more reliable than women. _____

_____

4. Allen and Irene do exactly the same work, but Allen is paid more. _____

_____

5. George, who is 50, applied for a job as a mechanic. The garage manager told George he wouldn't get the job because George is too old. _____

_____

What Rights Do Employees Have?

In most of the situations above, workers are protected from unfair treatment by their employers. That protection is guaranteed by federal laws.

Those same laws also guarantee employees certain basic rights. Some of those rights include:

♦ the right to a safe workplace
♦ the right to be free from sexual harassment
♦ the right to a job regardless of race, national origin, sex, age, handicaps, or religious or political beliefs
♦ the right to privacy

In addition to federal laws, there are many state and local laws that give workers more protection against unfair treatment by employers. Labor unions may provide even more protection for workers who are members. This extra protection is because labor unions and employers sign contracts that spell out workers' rights. These contracts state what employers can expect from workers and how the workers can expect to be treated. Employers are legally required to abide by their contracts with labor unions.

Fair Treatment

All of the situations at the beginning of the section involve the unfair, illegal treatment of employees. There are many other situations that take place at work that, while they are not illegal, seem to be unfair. An employer who is fair follows some basic principles of employee relations. They include:

♦ paying promptly
♦ explaining a worker's duties and the procedures for carrying them out
♦ notifying a worker about any changes in responsibilities or in procedures
♦ giving a worker **performance reviews** at scheduled times
♦ informing workers about chances for advancement in the company
♦ providing any training needed to do the job

If you feel that you are being treated unfairly, talk to your supervisor. Explain the situation and ask for your supervisor's help or advice. If your supervisor can't or won't help you, talk to someone in the human resources department. For example, if your company normally gives performance reviews every year and that time has passed without you getting yours, you are within your rights to ask when you can expect your performance review.

Getting Fair Treatment

1. A co-worker comes to you with a problem. She tells you that she didn't receive a paycheck as scheduled. She asks you for advice on what to do. What would you advise?

_____
_____
_____
_____

2. You recently started a new job as a secretary. Your boss has asked you to do personal chores for him, such as balancing his checkbook and buying gifts for his wife. What would you do?

_____
_____
_____
_____

What Rights Do Employers Have?

As an employer, Mel also has rights and **expectations**. He can expect certain things from workers. For example, Mel has the right to expect each employee to put in a full day's work for a full day's pay. That means his workers should report to work on time and do the work they're assigned without being told. It also means that Mel's employees should observe the time limits for breaks and work steadily until quitting time.

If a worker is absent from work without a

good reason, or if he or she arrives late or leaves early, Mel may subtract money from his or her pay for the time lost. In some cases, Mel has the right to fire employees for excessive lateness or absence.

When you accept a job, you are agreeing to try to satisfy your employer's expectations. In the overall performance of your job, your employer has the right to expect you to be:

♦ **capable**
♦ **cooperative**
♦ **honest**
♦ **loyal**
♦ **polite**
♦ **reliable**

In most cases, an employer may fire you if you break the terms of the contract between you and your employer. In addition, you may also be fired if you fail to follow the policies in your company manual. It's important to be familiar with these policies. For example, suppose your employee manual states that employees may have 10 sick days a year. If you have missed only nine days and your employer threatens to fire you for taking too many sick days, you can point out the policy that is written in the employee manual.

Safe Working Conditions

Under federal law, all workers are guaranteed the right to a safe workplace. This law, the Occupational Safety and Health Act, aims to protect employees at work by setting safety and health standards. For example, to ensure safety in factories, machinery should be in good running condition. Protective gear should be provided for workers who use machinery that can pose a threat to health and safety.

As a part of this law, employers must tell workers about any hazardous materials, such as asbestos or other cancer-causing materials, in the workplace. The materials must be properly labeled, and precautions for handling them must be clearly explained.

If you encounter hazards at work, tell your supervisor or employer about them immediately. If the condition isn't corrected, you should contact the Occupational Safety and Health Administration (OSHA). This federal agency enforces standards for job safety. It will make sure the law is carried out by sending an inspector to look at the conditions. If the law is being broken, the inspector may order an employer to correct hazards. Keep in mind that if you have to contact OSHA to report hazardous conditions, the law says that employers cannot fire you for doing so.

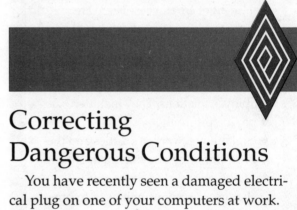

Correcting Dangerous Conditions

You have recently seen a damaged electrical plug on one of your computers at work. Who would you tell about it? _____

_____

If, after a few weeks, nothing had been done to fix the plug, what would you do?

_____

_____

_____

Now look in your phone book to see if you can locate the phone numbers of organizations that deal with job-related health or safety problems. Write the names of up to two government agencies below, along with their phone numbers.

Name: _____

Phone number: _____

Name: _____

Phone number: _____

Sexual Harassment

Federal laws protect workers not only from unsafe conditions but also from certain kinds of mistreatment on the job. For example, **sexual harassment**, which includes improper advances or remarks from supervisors or co-workers, is against the law.

The federal Equal Employment Opportunity Commission (EEOC) defines sexual harassment as including sexual advances or other behavior of a sexual nature if:

♦ a worker must go along with this behavior to keep the job

♦ an employer's decisions about an applicant or worker are based on how the person responds to advances or other sexual behavior

♦ the sexual behavior creates an unfriendly or difficult work environment or interferes with an employee's ability to do work.

Identifying sexual harassment can be difficult. Different people have different ideas about what sexual harassment is. For instance, someone who asks a co-worker for a date or makes a sexual joke may not be harassing the co-worker.

If, however, you feel that you are being harassed at work, it is important that you file a complaint immediately. Find out if the business you work for has a formal procedure for handling complaints. If it does, file your complaint according to this procedure first.

If your employer doesn't correct the problem after you complain about it, or if your company has no formal procedure, then file a complaint with the EEOC or the Fair Employment Practices Commission (FEPC). Both commissions will review the facts and determine if sexual harassment has taken place. When reviewing the case, the EEOC will consider how quickly the worker filed a

Discrimination can be difficult to pinpoint. If you suspect that you're being discriminated against, go to a civil rights agency.

formal complaint with the employer or with the EEOC.

The EEOC will also consider whether the person who made the advance or remark has authority over the worker whom he or she offended. If it was made by someone who has the power to hire, fire, or promote the worker, a court could order the employer to make changes to correct the problem and pay the worker for the damage suffered.

Discrimination

In Section 5 you learned that, by law, employers cannot discriminate against you when you apply for jobs. The same is true at work—employers cannot discriminate against employees on the job.

There are many forms of discrimination. Discrimination may be racial, religious, or political. Or discrimination may be based on national origin, gender, sexual orientation, age, or handicaps. Racial discrimination is one of the most common forms. For example, when an employer doesn't promote workers because they are black, racial discrimination is taking place. Equal employment opportunity laws require that employers base their decisions about hiring and promotions on qualifications, such as skills, education, or general ability.

For Help with Discrimination

If you feel that you are a victim of discrimination, you can file a complaint with the EEOC, the federal Civil Rights Commission, or a state civil rights agency. A number of non-government organizations also help

(continued)

workers who have been treated unfairly. One of them is the American Civil Liberties Union (ACLU). Lawyers from this organization represent people who file lawsuits against employers for discrimination.

The National Association for the Advancement of Colored People (NAACP) is a nongovernment organization that defends blacks against discrimination. And, if you have questions about employment laws that protect women against discrimination, you can call 9 to 5, National Association of Working Women, toll free at 1-800-245-9865.

Handling Discrimination at Work

Suppose that you are in your fifties and you have worked for the same company for 15 years. You have been passed over several times for a promotion, while less experienced people in their thirties have been promoted. You believe that your employer is discriminating against you because of your age. What would you do? _____

_____

_____

Now look in your phone book to see if you can find the phone numbers of organizations that fight discrimination. Write the names of up to two organizations and their phone numbers on the lines that follow.

Name: _____

Phone number: _____

Name: _____

Phone number: _____

Your employer has the right to look in or search through your belongings at work, unless you keep them locked up.

Privacy

Workers also have the right to a reasonable degree of privacy on the job. For example, if your employer permits you to lock your desk, locker, or filing cabinets and does not have keys to them, you can generally assume that they will not be searched. If, on the other hand, you don't have locks on your desk, locker, or filing cabinets, then your employer has the right to search those places.

Some aspects of privacy in the workplace have caused much disagreement, or **controversy**. One sensitive issue involves requiring workers to take polygraph (lie detector) tests.

Employers may require applicants and employees to take polygraph tests for many reasons. For example, if company-owned equipment has been stolen, then the company may want to question employees by using a polygraph test.

However, there are many problems with polygraph tests. The main problem is that the results of these tests are not always reliable. Courts of law usually won't accept polygraph test results as evidence. And several states ban the use of the polygraph during the application process because they feel it invades applicants' privacy.

Another controversy concerns **monitoring** employees while they work on computers. This is particularly true in the telecommunications industry, involving telephone operators' placing of calls. When a worker uses a computer that is part of an electronic network, a supervisor can use another computer in the network to watch and check the worker's performance.

Some employers claim that they need to do this to measure employees' **productivity**, or the amount of work employees produce. But some employee groups claim that this practice invades workers' privacy and increases stress. So far, there are no federal or state laws against doing this.

Other work-related controversies include testing for the AIDS virus and drugs. We will discuss those issues next.

If you believe that your right of privacy is being invaded at work, contact the ACLU or another civil rights group in your area.

Testing for the AIDS Virus and Contagious Diseases

A controversial privacy issue involves testing workers for the virus that causes acquired immune deficiency syndrome, or AIDS. AIDS is a disease for which there currently is no cure. AIDS destroys the immune system and eventually leads to death. AIDS is transmitted only through certain body fluids.

People get AIDS mainly through practicing unsafe sex or by sharing infected hypodermic needles. Some people have also gotten AIDS by receiving transfusions with infected blood. A few health care workers report that they have gotten AIDS through accidental contact with infected needles or patients' blood. However, you cannot catch AIDS merely by working with someone who has it.

AIDS is a serious problem for the workplace. Treatment for AIDS costs tens of thousands of dollars per person. The number of people with AIDS continues to increase. This affects medical insurance costs and benefits as well as company profits.

Because of the high medical treatment costs of the disease, some employers require that job applicants or workers be tested for HIV, commonly known as the AIDS virus. Other employers ask that workers volunteer to take these tests.

People with AIDS must often deal with discrimination. In the United States, AIDS is most common in homosexual men, drug users, and their sexual partners. Some of the discrimination against people with AIDS results from the negative feelings some people have towards homosexuals and drug users. Discrimination also results because many people don't understand what AIDS is and how it spreads.

While employers may have good reasons for testing workers for the virus, many people believe that this testing breaks the law by invading their privacy. If you carry the virus, or if an employer requires that you be tested for it, your rights depend on the laws in the state where you work. Most states have laws that require you to sign a form before your blood can be tested. Those laws also require that the results of the test be kept secret.

Most states treat AIDS as they treat other diseases and handicaps. In these states, an employer cannot fire or refuse to hire a worker simply because he or she has AIDS. If you feel that you have been discriminated against, contact a civil rights organization. Some legal authorities believe that job discrimination against people with AIDS is illegal throughout the United States.

Drug Testing

The controversy of drug testing is another employee privacy issue. More and more employers are using drug tests to discourage drug and alcohol abuse by workers. Some people believe that drug tests invade workers' privacy. Others feel that the tests are needed to make sure the workplace is safe.

The U.S. Supreme Court has ruled that drug testing of some employees, such as railroad workers and some federal government employees, is legal. This testing includes workers whose jobs involve law enforcement or public safety. For other jobs, there are no federal laws for or against drug testing by employers, although some states and cities have passed laws that place limits on it. An employer may ask you for samples of your blood and urine to test for drugs as part of a medical exam before you start a job. Some companies also test all employees for drugs during scheduled medical exams. Or they may test employees from time to time without advance notice. An employer may request drug tests for a worker who has been involved in an accident on the job or who has been acting strangely at work.

Employers test workers for drug use because people under the influence of drugs can be dangerous to themselves and to others. An employer is legally required to provide a safe workplace. Drug testing can help them meet this requirement. In addition to safety problems, drug abuse by workers can lead to work-related problems, such as lower productivity, poor attitudes about work, and theft or other dishonest behavior.

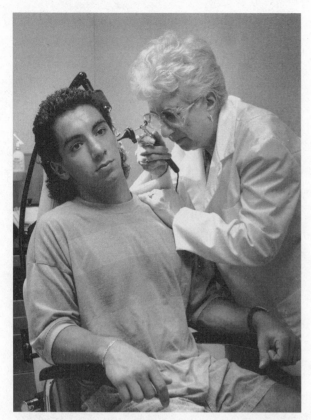

In some companies, agreeing to take a drug test is a condition for employment and can be part of the pre-employment medical exam.

If you agree to take a drug test, the medical worker who takes your samples should seal them with special tape so no one can touch them. That should be done in front of you. A lab will test the fluids for evidence of illegal or prescription drugs. Some drugs, including marijuana, can show up as long as 28 days after they are used. Other drugs only remain in the blood or urine for a few days.

Drug tests aren't always accurate. If a test indicates that your blood or urine contains drugs, you should be given a second test to check this finding.

If you're applying for a job and a drug test shows that you have used illegal drugs, such as marijuana or cocaine, an employer can legally refuse to hire you. If you're already working for an employer and you take a drug test that shows that you have used illegal drugs, you can be fired or referred to a drug-abuse treatment program.

If the tests show that you have used prescription drugs, such as tranquilizers, that affect you mentally and physically, you may be asked to get a letter from your doctor that explains why you're taking them. Even if you're using a prescription drug under a doctor's orders, the employer may refuse to hire you if use of the drug on the job could be dangerous to your safety or to the safety of others you work with.

More Employee Rights

Several other federal laws and regulations protect workers' rights and establish employment practices. The Fair Labor Standards Act sets minimum wages and maximum hours for most jobs. It also establishes employees' rights to extra pay for overtime. And it sets limits on the work children may do.

This law lets employers consider tips as part of your wages, along with the cost of any housing that the employer provides. The Fair Labor Standards Act covers most jobs. Your state employment office can tell you whether your job is covered by this law.

The federal government requires some offices to take **affirmative action** to hire women, members of racial and ethnic minority groups, and others who have been discriminated against in the past.

Under affirmative action, employers must try to hire members of these groups. This helps to ensure that women, minority group members, and the handicapped are given a chance to enter all types of jobs.

Where to Find Help

In this section, you learned where to go for help in a lot of different situations.

Read the situations below and list one place you could go for help in solving the problem.

1. You have discovered that your company is storing hazardous chemicals in the basement. You told your employer, but he said to mind your own business. You're concerned about safety in your building. Where would you go for help?

   _____

   _____

   _____

2. You are a member of a labor union. As part of the union's contract with your employer, you should be paid double-time when you work overtime. However, your employer says that you don't have this right. Where would you go for help?

   _____

   _____

   _____

3. The only people getting promoted in your company are of the opposite sex. You have been passed over for a promotion several times. The people who got promotions had less skill and experience. Where would you go for help?

   _____

   _____

   _____

4. Your company recently bought new equipment. You have been told that you must use that equipment today, but you haven't been trained to use it. Where would you go for help?

   _____

   _____

   _____

5. Your supervisor has threatened to fire you unless you grant him sexual favors. You work in a small company that doesn't have a procedure for handling these types of complaints. Where would you go for help?

   _____

   _____

   _____

6. You always lock your locker at work. Your employer doesn't have a key to it. When you came to work today, your supervisor had opened your locker and found application forms for other jobs. He is threatening to fire you. Where would you go for help?

   _____

   _____

   _____

Points to Remember

In this section, you learned that employers expect to get a full day's work for a full day's pay. In return, employees have certain rights and expectations. Some of the most important ones include:

♦ the right to a safe workplace
♦ the right to work free from sexual harassment
♦ the right to a job or chance for promotion regardless of race, national origin, gender, sexual orientation, age, handicaps, or religious or political beliefs
♦ the right to privacy

Word-Wise

Fill in the blanks below to explain some important points about workers' rights. The answers are key terms introduced in this section.

1. Employers with _____ _____ programs look for minority workers.

2. The disagreement or _____ over drug testing has to do with the right of privacy.

3. Drug use in the workplace can lead to lower _____.

4. If workers don't meet an employer's _____, they may be fired.

5. A supervisor who refuses to promote a worker who won't go out with him may be guilty of _____ _____.

Putting It to Work

You have a friend who is starting her first job. She has asked you to explain what she should do to meet her employer's expectations. List four things you would tell her.

1. _____

_____

2. _____

_____

3. _____

_____

4. _____

_____

You Be the Judge

You are applying for a job. The employer has asked you to take a drug test. What would you do? _____

_____

_____

If you take the test, how can you help to make sure it's accurate? _____

_____

_____

If you take the test and it turns out positive, what would you do? _____

_____

_____

Getting the Facts

Choose one right guaranteed an employee from this section that you would like to learn more about. Write it on the line below.

Right: _____

Then go to the library or read articles you may have at home to find out more about this employee right. Write a few sentences explaining what you learned.

_____

_____

_____

_____

_____

Does this affect you now? _____
If so, how? _____

_____

_____

What was the source of your information?

_____

_____

SUCCEEDING AT WORK

Tanya was sitting in Ms. Ford's office. Tanya had been a nursing assistant at the hospital for six months, and it was time for her first performance review.

"In general, Tanya, I'm very pleased with your work," Ms. Ford said.

"Thank you," Tanya said, smiling.

"You're prompt, you work hard, and you're intelligent. I know that I only have to explain something to you once, and you'll be able to do it well," Ms. Ford said. "And the patients like you."

"I like them a lot," Tanya said.

"I could tell that you liked to be with people when I hired you," Ms. Ford said. "And you work well with the staff. However, sometimes I think that you socialize a little too much. Be careful not to let it interfere with your work."

"OK, Ms. Ford," Tanya said. "I'll do that."

"Now, do you have any questions or problems?" Ms. Ford asked.

"There is one problem I want to talk to you about," Tanya said. "I'm having trouble working with Kathy. She interrupts me in the middle of my work to ask me the same questions over and over. At first I didn't mind, but now it's starting to get to me."

"I'm very glad you told me about this before it becomes a big problem," Ms. Ford said. "Have you suggested that Kathy ask me questions?"

"Yes," Tanya answered. "But she doesn't want to bother you. She thinks you're too busy."

"Tanya, I'll speak to Kathy about that," Ms. Ford said. "But try to be patient and help out Kathy when she asks you questions. After all that's what nursing is all about—helping people and working as a team."

"All right, Ms. Ford," Tanya said. "I'll do my best."

Guidelines for Success

Tanya's supervisor was pleased with Tanya's performance. Tanya performed well because she had good work habits and a positive attitude. Those are qualities that employers want to see, and those same qualities can lead to success on the job.

Succeeding in your work means getting the work done to the best of your ability. In addition, people who are really successful have positive attitudes about their jobs and their employers. They make an effort to communicate with their supervisors, as Tanya did. And they respect and cooperate with their co-workers.

Success on the job depends on small things, too. Your work habits may seem like minor details, but they do affect your performance and the performance of your co-workers. Let's take a look at the work habits that can help you succeed.

♦ **Be on time.** Get to work at the scheduled time, or even a few minutes early. Being late may affect the work of others. Return from lunch and breaks on time, too. If you can't avoid being late or absent, call your supervisor.

♦ **Follow rules and directions.** Every company and every department has its own way of doing things so it runs smoothly, safely, and productively. Those rules and directions have been made for a particular reason, so follow them.

♦ **Be reliable.** Be ready to perform whatever tasks you're given. And complete your work on time.

♦ **Be accurate.** Try to do your work as correctly as possible. If you make an error, admit it and correct it if possible.

♦ **Be thorough.** Complete each job you start. Don't leave tasks unfinished. Ask for help if you need it.

♦ **Be flexible.** Be willing to do new tasks or to do tasks in a new way.

♦ **Cooperate with others.** Be polite and considerate of all the people you deal with at work.

♦ **Dress appropriately.** Wear clothes that meet your company's requirements.

In addition to work habits, your attitude affects your performance at work. If you have a positive attitude, you enjoy your work and try to find ways to do your job better. You look for the best in everything around you. If you have a negative attitude, you view work as an obligation and you do only what you have to in order to keep your job.

Employers value workers who have a positive attitude. Those employees are cheerful, cooperative, and considerate. Since they get along with their co-workers, they help the company run smoothly. Of course, not all of your co-workers will have positive attitudes. Try to choose friends at work who *do* have positive attitudes. Friends with negative attitudes may eventually create a negative attitude in you as well.

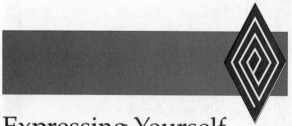

Expressing Yourself Positively

Many people don't realize the impression they make. They may think they have a positive attitude. But the things they say may actually seem negative to others.

Read the negative statements below. Then rework them so they sound positive. Read the example before you begin.

Negative: I can't learn how to do that by tomorrow.
Positive: I will do my best to learn that by tomorrow.

1. I won't do that because it's not part of my job.

_____

_____

_____

2. It's not my fault she made that mistake.

_____

_____

_____

3. That's his problem, not mine.

_____

_____

_____

4. I don't want to help him. He's just slow because he's disorganized.

_____

_____

_____

Failing to Succeed at Work

Bad habits and poor attitudes are the main reasons employers fire their workers. The following specific reasons are those most commonly given:

♦ **not following directions or company rules**
♦ **being dishonest**
♦ **stealing from the company**
♦ **being careless and making too many errors**
♦ **being unproductive**
♦ **not finishing tasks**
♦ **not getting along with others**
♦ **coming to work late or leaving early**
♦ **being absent from work too much**
♦ **taking too many breaks that are too long**
♦ **not being willing to learn new tasks**
♦ **not making the effort to improve**

Getting Along with Your Supervisor

The most important relationship you will have at work will be with your supervisor. In fact, that relationship will affect your success at work more than any other.

Your supervisor tells you how to do your job, answers your questions, helps you solve work-related problems, and checks your work. Supervisors also review your work performance at specific times during the year.

The keys to maintaining a good relationship with your supervisor are having a positive attitude, doing your job well, and communicating regularly. Your supervisor expects you to be dependable, capable, and cooperative. In addition, he or she expects you to ask questions or seek advice whenever necessary.

Tanya and Ms. Ford had a good working relationship. During Tanya's review, Ms. Ford praised Tanya's strengths and told her what she needed to change to improve her performance. Then Tanya brought up a problem she was having so that Ms. Ford could help her resolve it.

As with Tanya and Ms. Ford, two-way communication should exist between you and your supervisor. It is your supervisor's responsibility to tell you what you need to know to do your job well. He or she also needs to give you **feedback** about your work. That feedback may be in the form of an informal discussion or a scheduled performance review. At the same time, you need to keep your supervisor informed of your progress and of any problems you may have in performing your job.

Having a good working relationship with your supervisor can help make your job more enjoyable and more rewarding. It can also help you succeed on the job, since your supervisor usually has the power to promote you.

Reviewing a Working Relationship

The relationship that workers have with their supervisors affects their jobs in many ways. Reread the story at the beginning of this section. Then answer the questions below.

1. Why was Tanya's relationship with Ms. Ford good? _____
_____
_____

2. If you were Tanya, how would you have handled the situation with Kathy?
_____
_____
_____

3. What qualities did Ms. Ford show as Tanya's supervisor?_____
_____
_____

4. If you were Ms. Ford, what would you say to Kathy?
_____
_____
_____
_____

Getting Along with Co-Workers

Getting along with your co-workers affects your success at work. If you have a friendly relationship with your co-workers, you will be happier and more productive at work. Supervisors value employees who cooperate with others because they help to ensure that the department runs smoothly.

Tanya worked with many different people at the hospital, and she got along well with them. Ms. Ford noticed that and praised her for it.

Tanya was also supportive of her co-workers. She helped Kathy, even though Kathy kept interrupting her. And when Tanya felt that Kathy needed help, Tanya discussed it with Ms. Ford.

When you work with others as part of a team, it is essential that you get along with all the team members. In order to produce good work, your team must be able to communicate and cooperate. That's why Ms. Ford was concerned about the problem between Tanya and Kathy. Ms. Ford wanted her staff to know that she was always available to discuss work or answer questions.

Getting along with all types of people can be easier if you follow a few simple rules:

♦ Treat others the way you would like to be treated.

♦ Help others when they need it or when they ask for it.

♦ Show respect to workers who have more experience or more knowledge than you do.

♦ Be pleasant, polite, and considerate.

♦ Avoid talking about other people behind their backs.

♦ Avoid talking down to people or being overly critical.

♦ Choose your friends on the job for their positive attitudes.

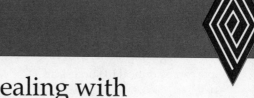

Dealing with Co-Workers

You will have to deal with many different situations at work. Many will involve co-workers. Practicing ahead of time can help.

Read the following and explain what you would do.

1. If a co-worker told you that she had a personal problem she wanted your advice on, what would you do?

_____

_____

2. If a co-worker asked you to help him out in a work crisis, what would you do?

_____

_____

3. If your two officemates spent so much time talking that you had trouble working, what would you do?

_____

_____

4. If a co-worker complained to you about unfair office policies, what would you do?

_____

_____

_____

Getting Along with Other People

Many people have to interact with customers, clients, or patients at work. Workers' relationships with these people are different from their relationships with co-workers. But, as with co-workers, getting along with these people can be critical to success at work.

Keep the following points in mind when you deal with customers, clients, or patients:

(continued)

♦ Treat customers, clients, or patients the way you would like to be treated.

♦ Live by the motto "Customers, clients, and patients are always right." That means you shouldn't argue or get angry with them, even if you know they're wrong.

♦ Regardless of the way you're treated or feel, remain pleasant, polite, and calm.

♦ Treat everyone with dignity, patience, and consideration.

♦ Avoid keeping people waiting too long, if possible. Apologize if you do.

♦ If a person causes too many problems, refer him or her to your supervisor or someone in management.

♦ Remember that your job may no longer exist if your customer or client isn't satisfied.

Solving Problems

When you have a problem at work, the best rule to follow is to make an effort to resolve it. Problems that aren't resolved can become bigger and cause tensions.

Tanya made an effort to resolve her problem by talking it over with Ms. Ford. Ms. Ford gave Tanya advice and told Tanya that she would talk to Kathy.

If you're having a problem with a co-worker, approach that person and talk about it. If your co-worker doesn't want to cooperate, or if you can't resolve your differences, discuss it with your supervisor.

Tanya tried to resolve the growing tension she felt toward Kathy by suggesting that Kathy ask Ms. Ford when Kathy had questions. When that discussion didn't solve the problem, Tanya talked to Ms. Ford. In that way, the problem didn't grow so big that it affected Tanya's performance. And Ms. Ford could talk to Kathy to change Kathy's impression that Ms. Ford was too busy to answer questions.

Whenever you encounter a problem that you can't handle, go to your supervisor. For example, if you discover that a co-worker is stealing, don't try to resolve the problem on your own. Situations such as this should usually be handled by someone who works in management.

You may also have problems with customers, clients, or patients. If you feel that you can't resolve them, consult your supervisor or someone in management. When you have to handle a problem yourself, perhaps because no one is available to help you, remain calm and try to be fair. You might want to ask the customer or client to leave a name and phone number so your supervisor can contact him or her later. If you have to handle a problem on your own, you may want to explain the details to your supervisor later.

How do you handle a problem that relates directly to your supervisor? If the problem is work-related or involves a minor personality conflict, talk to your supervisor. Supervisors have experience dealing with problems. And they want to do their best to keep their employees happy.

If you don't feel comfortable talking to your supervisor, or if the problem concerns discrimination or sexual harassment, you may want to talk to another supervisor or someone in your company's human resources department. See Section 9 for more information on handling issues related to employee rights.

Your supervisor can help you work out problems that you can't solve on your own.

Performance Reviews

Most workplaces schedule periodic evaluations of workers' performance. These evaluations provide supervisors and workers with the opportunity to assess performance and to discuss the department and the company. Procedures vary from company to company, and these reviews may be either informal or formal.

Tanya's discussion with Ms. Ford is an example of an informal performance review. Ms. Ford and Tanya talked about Tanya's strengths and weaknesses. And Tanya discussed the problem she was having.

Some companies have formal procedures for performance reviews. The worker and the supervisor may both fill out a form before discussing it. Or workers may fill out forms and then give them to supervisors to read and comment on. In other companies, the supervisors fill out forms and discuss them with individual employees.

When you are new to a job, your first few months at work may be considered a **probationary period**. That means that during that time your performance will be observed to determine whether you're capable of doing the work. At the end of the probationary period, your supervisor evaluates your performance. If you have performed well during the probationary period, you will become a regular employee.

Even after the probationary period is over, you should still get performance reviews. In many companies, employees are scheduled for reviews once a year. At that time, the employee's work is evaluated. Some companies give salary raises or promotions to workers who get good performance reviews.

No matter what type of job you have, you should have at least one performance review a year. If you're not sure what your company policy is, ask your supervisor or someone in the human resources department. Find out when performance reviews take place and what types of things will be evaluated.

Remember that a performance review is a two-way street. It is a time when you receive feedback from your supervisor. But it is also a time when you assess your role on the job and openly discuss your feelings about your job and the company.

You shouldn't be afraid of performance reviews. Instead, you should look forward to them. After all, performance reviews are chances for you to express your feelings, ask questions, find out what you're doing right and wrong, and learn how to improve your performance. Performance reviews are also opportunities for you to demonstrate your positive attitude.

What Will Be Evaluated?

Companies vary in the type of reviews and evaluation forms they use. But most companies use **criteria** similar to those on page 111 to evaluate workers. That means that workers' performances are measured against specific ideal standards.

Some of the most common criteria include:

♦ **Skill.** Has the worker consistently demonstrated a high level of skill and job knowledge?

♦ **Quality of work.** Is the employee's work accurate, neat, and thorough? Does he or she follow directions properly?

♦ **Quantity of work.** Does the worker use his or her time efficiently and effectively? Does he or she report to his or her supervisor when tasks are completed?

♦ **Reliability.** Does the worker complete work on time? Does he or she follow through on all assigned work? Does he or she work steadily, even with minimal supervision?

♦ **Dependability.** Does the worker follow company rules? Is he or she on time for work? Does he or she take only the allotted time for

PERFORMANCE REVIEW FORM

Employee Name (Last, First, Middle)	Employee No.	Title

Department	Location	How long has employee worked for you?

Rater's Name (Last, First, Middle)	Title

RATING SCALE

5 = Superior   Outstanding performance that greatly exceeds job requirements.

4 = Good   Performance meets job expectations and generally exceeds them.

3 = Adequate   Basic job requirements are being met.

2 = Poor   Performance is below job requirements.

1 = Unsatisfactory   Performance is unacceptable.

NO = Not observed   Performance not observed.

Circle the rating that most accurately describes the employee's performance for each of the areas listed.

RATING FACTORS	RATING (Circle one.)
TECHNICAL FACTORS—Consider the level of skill or job knowledge demonstrated by employee.	1 2 3 4 5 NO
WORK QUALITY—Consider neatness, accuracy, thoroughness, and how well employee grasps and follows instructions.	1 2 3 4 5 NO
WORK QUANTITY—Consider whether employee uses time efficiently and effectively.	1 2 3 4 5 NO
RELIABILITY—Consider employee's timely completion of tasks and follow-through on all tasks.	1 2 3 4 5 NO
ATTENDANCE—Consider punctuality, number of work days missed.	1 2 3 4 5 NO
COOPERATION—Consider employee's ability to get along and work well with others.	1 2 3 4 5 NO
PARTICIPATION—Consider employee's overall interest, initiative, and enthusiasm shown in work.	1 2 3 4 5 NO

COMMENTS

Comment on any rating that is Superior or Unsatisfactory. These comments should give examples of the employee's specific work performance and should illustrate how good or poor the performance is.

Rater's Signature	Date

On this review form, the criteria for evaluation include technical factors, work quality, work quantity, reliability, attendance, cooperation, and participation.

breaks and lunches? Does the worker take care of company property?

♦ **Dealing with people.** Does the worker respect authority? Does he or she get along with all types of co-workers? Does he or she work well as part of a team? Does he or she work well with customers, clients, or patients? Is the worker cooperative and pleasant to work with?

♦ **Initiative.** Does the worker have **initiative**, or like to take on new responsibilities and challenges? Does he or she make an effort to improve performance? Is the worker flexible?

Joining a Union

If you join a union, success on the job is not as closely linked to your relationship with your supervisor and your employer. In a union, your salary, raises, benefits, promotions, and working conditions are written down in a contract. That contract is approved by the members of the union and signed by the union leaders and the employer. The union **negotiates**, or works out, these terms for all the members.

Most contracts have some of the following sections:

♦ **Wages and fringe benefits.** Wages are based on the clearly defined job that each worker performs.

♦ **Workers' rights on the job.** Workers are given a voice in determining working conditions. They can complain about the conditions without fear of punishment. And they can object to firing decisions that are made without just cause.

Workers in unions may go on strike if they feel they're being denied their rights. What rights do you think these union members are striking for?

- **Union's rights regarding the employer.** The union has the right to represent its membership when bargaining with employers.
- **Employer's rights regarding the union.** The employer is given the right to manage the company, to establish reasonable rules, to hire, and to fire with just cause.
- **Union enforcement of rights.** The union has a system that handles workers' problems, or **grievances**, with the employer.

A union worker must follow the terms of the contract his or her union has signed with the employer. If union workers have management-related problems that their supervisors can't or won't solve, they should talk to the **shop steward**. The shop steward settles disputes between workers and management. The shop steward will present the worker's problem to the employer and then work out a solution.

Many union contracts state that a company must run a **closed shop**. That means that all workers must belong to the union and be included in the union contract. If you get a job with such a company, union dues are usually deducted from your gross salary.

Union membership has some advantages and some disadvantages. Unions are powerful negotiators for workers' rights, though their strength has weakened over the years. Unions also have the right to strike until a suitable contract is negotiated. And unions help workers financially during a strike. Unions may also provide workers with a **credit union**. This organization allows workers to borrow money at lower interest rates and save money at higher interest rates than many other financial institutions offer. Disadvantages of union membership include having to pay union dues and having to accept the union contract even if there are conditions that you don't like.

Before you join a union, talk to other members and union representatives. Find out how much union dues cost and what benefits you would receive. Being a union member may be one way for you to succeed at work.

Points to Remember

In this section, you learned that it is within your power to do many things to help you succeed at work. Some of the most important include:

- having good work habits
- having a positive attitude
- getting along with your supervisor
- getting along with co-workers
- understanding how to solve various types of problems
- preparing for performance reviews
- joining a union, when appropriate

CHECKPOINT

Word-Wise

Complete each sentence below by writing in the correct word or words. The answers are key terms introduced in this section.

1. Your first few months at a new job may be a _____ _____ during which the quality of your work is observed by your supervisor.

2. When all the workers in a company must belong to a union, it is called a _____ _____.

3. Your supervisor will review your performance based on specific _____.

4. When union members have problems, they

report their _____ to union representatives.

5. If union members have problems with working conditions, they would speak to the _____ _____ about it.

Putting It to Work

You have been at a new job for six months. You are scheduled to have your first performance review tomorrow morning. To prepare for the review, list five subjects you expect the supervisor to discuss with you.

1. _____
2. _____
3. _____
4. _____
5. _____

Now list three subjects you would like to discuss with your supervisor.

1. _____
2. _____
3. _____

You Be the Judge

You have found out that a co-worker is cheating on her timesheet. What would you do?

_____
_____
_____
_____
_____

Would you do anything differently if she were a close friend of yours? _____

If so, what would you do? _____

_____
_____
_____
_____

Getting the Facts

You have learned that you approach different people at work for information depending on the type of information you need and the circumstances. Read the statements below and indicate the person you would speak to in each case.

1. If you're having problems with a co-worker: _____

2. If you have questions about your job:
   _____

3. If you're having problems with your supervisor: _____

4. If you feel that your supervisor is harassing you: _____

5. If you want to know your company's policy on performance reviews: _____
   _____

6. If you work for a union and you're having problems with your supervisor: _____
   _____

7. If you're having problems with a customer, client, or patient: _____
   _____

S E C T I O N 11

MOVING UP THE LADDER

"Ms. Ling, do you have a minute? I need to speak to you about something," Ted asked his boss.

"Sure," Ms. Ling replied. "Come back after Paul takes over for you."

A few minutes later, Ted sat down in Ms. Ling's small office at the back of the convenience store.

"What can I do for you, Ted?" Ms. Ling asked.

"Well," Ted said, "I know that Lynn just quit. And I would like to ask you to consider me for the job of assistant manager."

"Do you think you could handle it?" Ms. Ling asked.

"I'm sure I could," Ted said. "I know all the stock. I've done inventory. And I've written up purchase orders."

"There's more to the job than that," Ms. Ling said. "You'd have to help set store policy and work schedules, supervise the workers, and handle complaints."

"I've done much of that," Ted said. "I know store policy. And when we've had problems getting enough people to work, I've helped Lynn plan a work schedule. As far as complaints go, I've always tried to handle them at the cash register, so Lynn didn't have to deal with them. The only thing I haven't done is supervise. But I think I work well with people. I know the employees here, and I

think I could supervise them."

"Actually, I've been thinking of you for the assistant manager's job myself," Ms. Ling said. "But I have to check with the district manager. He'll want to interview you himself before making a final decision."

"But you'll talk to him about me?" Ted asked.

"Absolutely," Ms. Ling replied. "I'll let you know when he wants to meet with you. And, in the meantime, keep up the good work."

What Are Your Job Goals?

When Ted started working as a clerk at the convenience store, he knew what his goals were. He planned to use that job as a starting point. His long-term goal was to move up within the store.

Ted's plan took shape the first time he was interviewed. He studied the people working in the store. And he noticed that the assistant manager was only a little older than he was. Ted believed that meant there were opportunities for young people there.

During his job interview with Ms. Ling, Ted asked how employees earned promotions and moved up to more important jobs. She explained that most people worked their way up with on-the-job experience.

The company often promoted people within a store, she explained. Customers liked dealing with the same employees over time.

Allowing people to move up into better jobs was a good way for the company to hold on to its valued employees.

When Ted started his job, he felt that he had a bright future there. This gave him the **motivation** to work hard. He wanted to get along with co-workers and customers, and to learn as much as he could about managing the store. Now that Lynn was leaving, his efforts might be rewarded.

Ted is a good example of someone who knows what he wants. He has goals. One of his goals is to do a good job so that he can be promoted. A promotion would mean more responsibility and more money. As he gets ahead, Ted will also find other benefits that come with promotions:

♦ **He will have higher status.** People look up to a person in a management position.

♦ **He will be more satisfied.** A manager usually does more interesting and challenging work.

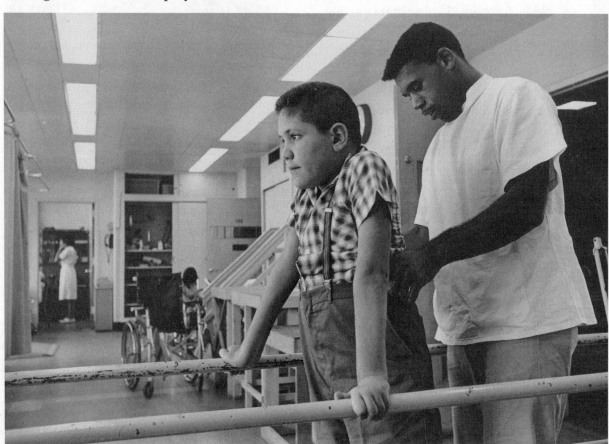

For many people, helping others is an important part of their job.

◆ **He will feel better about himself**. This increased **self-esteem** is one of the most important rewards of reaching career goals.

What do you want to get out of working? Most people work for money. But that's only part of the picture. Do you want to move up in the company, like Ted? Do you want to learn things on the job so you can earn a promotion? If so, where do you want that promotion to lead? It could lead to an even better job, to a management position, or to a job in a better company.

Different people have different hopes and dreams for their working lives. Some of the things people want from their jobs include opportunities to:

◆ **gain respect**
◆ **increase self-esteem**
◆ **help others**
◆ **improve the community**
◆ **learn more**
◆ **gain power**
◆ **travel**
◆ **have excitement**
◆ **be creative**

What Do You Want to Achieve?

Asking yourself what working means to you can help you figure out what your goals are and plan how to achieve them. Answer the questions below about working and setting goals.

1. What are the three things that are most important to you in a job?

_____

_____

_____

2. What is the first job you want to get? (If you are working now, describe the next job you want.)

_____

_____

_____

3. What are the three most important things you want from that job?

_____

_____

_____

4. Describe a job that you think would be better than the one you want to get.

_____

_____

_____

_____

5. Are you qualified for that job? _____ If not, how could you qualify? _____

_____

_____

6. What do you see yourself doing one year from now? _____

_____

_____

7. What do you see yourself doing five years from now? _____

_____

_____

8. On the lines below, describe your career plan. First, explain what your job goals are. Then list the steps you would take, on and off the job, to reach those goals. Your answers to questions 1 through 7 can help you.

_____

_____

_____

_____

_____

_____

_____

How to Ask for a Raise or Promotion

Most people want a job with opportunities for advancement. They like to know that they will be rewarded when they do good work.

Rewards usually come in the form of a raise or a promotion. When you get a raise, you're given more money for doing the same job. When you get a promotion, you're given a more responsible job. Usually, getting a promotion means getting a raise as well.

A promotion is a sign of a worker's success. Knowing that promotions are possible motivates people to put in extra effort. If you have a choice, avoid taking a job where promotions aren't possible.

Most companies are keen to promote good employees. And many give raises on a regular basis. But others don't offer promotions or raises. So you may have to ask.

Ted's approach is a good example of how to ask. Let's look at what he did right:

♦ **He asked for a chance to speak to his supervisor.** Instead of interrupting Ms. Ling's work, he waited until it was convenient for her to talk.

♦ **He chose a private place.** Ms. Ling's office was a good place to talk. The store would not have been, because people could overhear.

♦ **He picked the right time to make a request.** Since the assistant manager was leaving, Ted knew there was an opening.

♦ **He backed up his request.** Ted showed that he understood what was involved in doing the assistant manager's job and that he was qualified to do it.

A Manager's Role in Promotions

A smart manager knows the importance of allowing a good worker to get ahead. Ms. Ling was the type of manager who noticed her employee's efforts. She knew Ted was well qualified. She also liked the way he described his skills and experience. The fact that he didn't criticize any of the other employees who might be in competition for the job also worked in his favor.

Ms. Ling couldn't say yes to Ted's request for a promotion, because the district manager had the final say. Ms. Ling expected the district manager to go along with her plan. But there was a chance that he might say no. Why might this happen?

Suppose another convenience store owned by the same company burned down. The main office may have promised to place that store's assistant manager in the first available opening. Ted wouldn't get the job simply because it had been promised to someone else.

Whether Ted gets the promotion or not, asking is never a waste of time. Even if a promotion isn't possible this time, it's important for Ted's supervisor to know of Ted's **ambition**, or his interest in getting ahead. The new assistant manager may not work out. Or the company could open another store. Someone could transfer. Any one of these changes could result in Ted getting the promotion he wants.

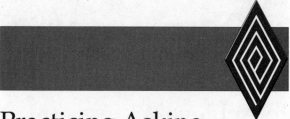

Practicing Asking for a Promotion

You have worked in the same job for a company for two or three years. You feel that your work is excellent and that you are ready to take on more responsibility. There is an opening for a job one level higher than yours. You have decided to ask for a promotion to that job.

Role-play this situation with another student. One person takes the role of the employee, and the other takes the role of the supervisor. Before you begin, be sure to decide what job you will have and what job you will be requesting a promotion to.

After you play one role, switch and try the other. Then answer the following questions.

1. How did you feel in the role of the employee?

    _____

    _____

2. What do you feel you did well?

    _____

    _____

3. What do you need to improve?

    _____

    _____

4. How could you make that improvement?

    _____

    _____

5. What advice would you give to your role-play partner when he or she played the employee?

    _____

    _____

    _____

How to Get Promoted

What makes a worker promotable? When you answer that question, think about Ted. He earned a promotion by doing his job, taking on extra responsibility, and working well with people. These are three very valuable qualities. But there are other qualities that are important as well.

Employers want employees who can contribute to the company's success. Here are some general do's and don'ts for getting promoted.

DO...

♦ Carry out all your job tasks carefully and correctly.

♦ Follow the company's rules.

♦ Come in on time and work a full day and a full week.

♦ Keep yourself and your work space neat and safe.

♦ Show that you care about the company and the product or service.

♦ Learn about the job and grow with it.

♦ Volunteer to take on extra responsibility.

♦ Get along with your co-workers and supervisor.

DON'T...

♦ Make anyone's job harder.

♦ Break rules or fall into careless habits.

♦ Cause problems between other people.

♦ Cheat or steal.

♦ Refuse to change or to take on new tasks.

♦ Let personal problems interfere with your job.

If you follow all of these tips for job success, you might get a promotion without asking for it. When a supervisor or employer clearly sees excellent job performance, he or she may decide to do something about it. The more good work you do, the greater the chances are that this will happen.

When You Can't Get Ahead

If you are doing your best work, but you can't seem to get ahead, the problem can lie with the company, with management, or with you. Ask yourself the following questions to see if the problem is a result of something you are or aren't doing.

♦ Do I have a positive attitude about my work?

♦ Am I really doing my best work?

♦ Have I improved in the position since I've had it?

If you lack the skills you need to get ahead, look for ways to get more training or education. You may be able to get the skills in evening classes.

♦ Am I good at solving problems?

♦ Do I make or save money for the company?

♦ Am I letting my strengths show?

♦ Am I working to strengthen my weak points?

♦ Do I come up with good ideas for handling my job?

♦ Do I go to my boss when I have problems I can't handle?

♦ Do I have all the skills or training I need to move up in the company?

If you answered no to any of these questions, work on improving yourself in these areas. And make sure the people you work with can see these improvements taking place. Ask for feedback from those you work for.

If the problem is a lack of skills, look for ways to get the training you need. Ask your supervisor about company training programs. Find out about evening classes offered through the local school system. Your company might even pay for them.

Your work may be excellent, but the company may not offer any rewards. Not all companies operate fairly. Certain people may be moved up, while others just as qualified are passed over. Or the company may be having financial problems. In this case, keeping costs down might be very important to management.

If you think that the problem lies with management, keep doing your best work. Don't complain to co-workers, or it may get back to your boss.

Finally, there may not be an opening above your present job. Most companies are organized so that as you move up, the number of job possibilities goes down. When you think you've gone as far as you can in your company, it may be time to look for a new job.

Seeking a New Job

Changing jobs may be one way to advance. The average worker in the United States spends only about three and a half years in one job. Many workers leave jobs to go to better ones.

Before you decide to leave one job, it's best to line up another, especially since you don't know how long it will take you to find a new job. If you quit your existing job without having another, you may have trouble meeting your obligations.

When you look for a new job, you will go through many of the same steps you followed on your first job hunt. You will read the help-wanted ads, make personal contacts, find out information about companies, and go on interviews.

This time there will be one important difference. You will have new work experience. That experience may or may not be enough to help you get the job you want. That depends on the work you have done so far, the skills you've acquired, and the recommendations you have.

When you decide to change jobs, try to keep your decision to yourself. If your supervisor finds out about your plans before you're ready to leave, you may risk losing your present job.

Read the help-wanted ads and make your telephone calls on your own time, not during your work hours. Use personal time to go on interviews. Keep up your good habits. Remember that it may take some time to find a new job.

Is It Time for a Change?

Before you decide whether it's time for you to change jobs, you should ask yourself some questions.

♦ Do I still have the same career goals I had when I took my present job?

♦ Do I need to change jobs in order to reach the goals I have?

♦ Have I explored every chance for moving up at my present company?

♦ Did I get enough experience to qualify for a better job at another company?

♦ Do I have the training or skills to get a better job?

♦ Have I worked at this job long enough to get good recommendations?

♦ Will a new job give me a chance for more growth and better pay?

If you answered yes to every question, then you're probably ready to change jobs. But if you answered no to several of the questions, then you may want to reevaluate your plans.

Instead of making a move, it might be better to put in some more time where you are. Look into training programs. Search for ways to make the job more interesting. Reevaluate your career goals. If you put more into the job you have now, you may be able to get more out of the next one.

What to Do If You're Laid Off or Fired

There may be times when you are let go from a job. If the economy is in bad shape and business is slow, or if your employer is doing poorly, you may be laid off. A **layoff** can be a temporary or permanent end to employment. Employers usually order layoffs for economic reasons. If business improves, workers who were laid off may be hired back.

Being laid off is not the same as being fired. Firing is the permanent dismissal of a worker. People who are fired are let go because they lack the necessary skills or work habits.

If you are fired or laid off, you should apply for **unemployment benefits**. You can do this at your local office of employment security. These benefits include weekly pay for people who lose their jobs through no fault of their own. You may receive these payments for up to six months. The length of time covered and the amount you receive vary from state to state.

Your local office of employment security will decide whether you should receive benefits. The decision depends on how long you worked and on the reason you were let go. You won't receive benefits if you quit your job without good cause or if you were fired for good cause.

If you were fired, try to learn from the experience. Find out what the problem was. Then do what you can to correct the problem so that you can succeed in your next job. For example, if you couldn't do the work, think about ways to build on your skills. If you had poor work habits, think about how you can improve them. Then be prepared to explain this on your next job interview.

If you were fired from a job, don't be discouraged. Think positively and start to look for a new job right away. Many people who lose their jobs find new ones that they are more suited to and like better.

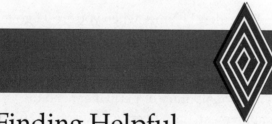

Finding Helpful Information

Use your local telephone book to find out the name, address, and telephone number of the office of employment security nearest you.

Name of office: _____

Address: _____

Phone number: _____

Resigning

If you decide to leave your job, try to do so on a positive note. The way you **resign**, or quit, is important. After all, you may want to return to the company one day. Or you may want to ask your supervisor or another manager to recommend you for another position elsewhere.

Inform your supervisor of your plan to leave your job as soon as you know you're leaving. This may be difficult, especially if you like your job, your supervisor, and the company you work for. But the sooner your supervisor knows, the more time he or she has to find someone to replace you. As a rule, you should try to give at least two weeks' notice before you leave.

Some employers ask valuable workers to reconsider leaving. They may offer employees more money or a promotion if they stay. If that happens, you must weigh the pros and cons to decide if you would rather stay or go. Consider the offer and how staying will affect your career plan and your goals.

After you inform your supervisor that you're leaving, follow up with a letter of resignation. See the box on page 123 for tips on how to write one.

When you resign, some firms require an "exit interview" for you to explain why you're leaving. This interview may be done by your supervisor or a human resources employee. This might help your company or department to change a condition or correct a problem that may be affecting other people in the office.

After you turn in your resignation, keep doing your best work. On your last day, return your keys, clear out your work space, and sign all the necessary papers. Ask for a letter of recommendation to take with you. Make sure the company has your correct address on file in case someone needs to ask you a question or send you something.

```
                                          123 Whitney Road
                                          Salem, NY 11223
                                          May 2, 199X


        Ms. Kim Ling, Manager
        Quick-Stop Market
        66 Broadway
        Salem, NY 11223

        Dear Ms. Ling:

           I am writing to tell you that I am
        resigning from my job as assistant manager of
        the Broadway Quick-Stop Market.

           My last day of work will be May 18, 199X.
        In June I will be getting married and moving to
        Orlando, Florida.

           I appreciate all the things you have
        taught me about managing a convenience store. I
        will miss working with you and the other store
        employees. I would be happy to help train my
        replacement during the next two weeks before I
        leave.

                           Yours truly,

                           Lynn Holden

                           Lynn Holden
```

Writing a Letter of Resignation

Follow these guidelines when you write a letter of resignation:

♦ Make the letter short and polite.
♦ Include the date you're leaving.
♦ Never criticize your supervisor or co-workers, even if you had problems with them.
♦ Explain your reason for leaving. If necessary, say that you need to pursue other career interests, rather than make negative comments.
♦ Thank your employer for the chance to work with the company.
♦ Say briefly why the job was a good experience.
♦ Offer to train your replacement.

Look at the example above. This is the letter that Lynn Holden wrote to Ms. Ling when she resigned from her job at the convenience store.

Practice Writing a Letter of Resignation

You have been working at Video Mart, a local videotape rental store, for two years. Your supervisor is Herman Brown. You've enjoyed the job and have learned a lot, including how to use a computer database.

Now you're leaving to take a job with a company that sells videos to stores like Video Mart all over the country.

On a separate sheet of paper, write a letter of resignation to your boss at Video Mart.

Getting Recommendations

When you look for a new job, employers will often ask you for references or letters of recommendation. These show new employers how former employers rate you as a

```
                          Quick-Stop Market
                          66 Broadway
                          Salem, NY 11223
                          May 18, 199X

To Whom It May Concern:

  Lynn Holden has worked at the Quick-Stop
Market from June 1989 until today. She held the
position of clerk for the first 14 months of
her employment. She was then promoted to her
present job of assistant manager. The
requirements of this job include overseeing
inventory, purchasing, setting store policy,
organizing work schedules, supervising workers,
and handling complaints.

  Lynn is an outstanding worker. She learns
quickly and is eager to take on more
responsibility. She gets along well with
customers and staff. She is reliable, careful,
and honest.

  As manager of the Quick-Stop Market and
Lynn's direct supervisor, I highly recommend
her for an assistant manager's job or another
similar position. Everyone at Quick-Stop Market
is sorry to see her go.

                          Very truly yours,

                          Kim Ling

                          Kim Ling
                          Manager
```

worker. Getting a good reference is one reason why you want to leave former employers on good terms.

When you leave a job, ask your supervisor or employer to write a letter of recommendation for you. If you were fired, however, don't ask for one.

After you give notice, make the request for a letter of recommendation as soon as possible. That way, the memory of your good work will still be fresh in everyone's mind. If you wait too long, the person you've asked may not have time. And if you wait until after you've left, your boss may also have gone on to another job. The letter that Kim Ling wrote on page 124 is a good example of a letter of recommendation.

A letter of recommendation should include the following basic information:

♦ your name and the name of the company you worked for

♦ the name and title of the person writing the letter

♦ the dates of your employment

♦ the fact that you worked well for the person writing the letter

♦ a description of the job's responsibilities

♦ several of your strongest skills or greatest accomplishments on the job

♦ a rating of your performance, from good to excellent

Before you ask for a letter of recommendation, find out if there is a company policy about who should write it. If there is, ask the correct person. It may be your supervisor, your employer, or the head of personnel. If you have more than one supervisor, you might be able to ask each one to write a letter. Just be sure that each writer knows you and the quality of your work.

If someone turns down your request for a letter, try to find out why. Your supervisor may not have the time or may dislike writing letters. In that case, ask if you can write one, and then he or she will simply have to read the letter and sign it. Another option is to ask to use your supervisors as references. If they say no, drop the subject and get someone else to recommend you.

Points to Remember

In this section, you learned that you can do many things to help yourself advance at work and move on to new jobs. In general, it's a good idea to:

♦ decide what your job goals are

♦ use the right approach to get a raise or promotion

♦ know when you've outgrown your present job and should look for a new one

♦ apply for unemployment benefits if you've lost your job

♦ resign from a job in a positive way

♦ get letters of recommendation to help you when you apply for new jobs

✓ C H E C K P O I N T ✓

Word-Wise

Complete each sentence below by writing in the correct word or words. The answers are key terms introduced in this section.

1. _____ _____ are payments to people who have lost their jobs.

2. To _____ means to quit a job.

3. When you feel good about yourself, you have high _____.

4. Workers who are very determined to do their job have _____.

5. If you have _____, then you're interested in getting ahead.

Putting It to Work

Suppose you have just been promoted. One of your new responsibilities is to talk about the company to new employees who have been hired at your old job level. Make a list of five suggestions you would give them to help them succeed.

1. _____

2. _____

3. _____

4. _____

5. _____

You Be the Judge

You have been employed at the same company for two and a half years. You think you have been doing your best work, but no one seems to notice. Recently, a co-worker who joined the company six months after you did was given a raise and moved to an area of the plant with better working conditions. You want to move up in the company too, and you feel frustrated that nothing has happened yet. What would you do?

_____

_____

_____

_____

Getting the Facts

Talk to someone you know who has been working for several years and who has received at least one promotion or who has changed jobs in order to advance. Ask this person the following questions. Then write down his or her answers.

1. What was your first job? _____

_____

2. What did you do in that job? _____

_____

_____

3. How did you feel about that job?

_____

_____

4. What were the most important things you learned on that job? _____

_____

_____

5. At what point did you feel that you were ready for a better job? _____

_____

6. What did you do when you felt that way?

_____

_____

7. Did your first efforts to get a better job work out? _____

Why or why not? _____

_____

8. What happened next? _____

_____

9. What did you learn from that experience?

_____

_____

10. How did you go from your first job to the job you have now? _____

_____

_____

11. Have your job goals changed since you started out? _____

If so, how? _____

_____

12. What do you want to accomplish next in your work life? _____

_____

_____

13. What advice would you give to people who are just starting to work? _____

_____

_____

GLOSSARY

A

adjustment period—time for learning to adapt to new routines and new people

adjustment test—a test that determines whether a person has the personal traits a job requires; also called a personality test

affirmative action—a policy whereby employers make a special effort to hire women, members of racial and ethnic minorities, and others who have been discriminated against in the past

allowance—on a Form W-4, the amount that can be deducted for each person, including the employee, who depends on the employee for support

ambition—an aim to succeed or gain a particular goal

application letter—a letter that aims to persuade an employer to interview an applicant for a job

apprentice—an on-the-job trainee who earns wages while learning a trade

aptitude—a natural ability or talent

aptitude test—a test that measures a person's natural abilities for performing and learning certain kinds of tasks

asset—something a person has to offer an employer, such as a talent, basic skill, technical skill, or education

association—an organization or group of persons who have common goals or interests

B

background skill—a skill used in many areas of life that can help you on the job

basic skill—a basic ability, such as reading, writing, and doing math

beneficiary—a person named to receive money from an insurance policy if an employee covered by the policy dies

blind ad—a help-wanted ad that does not include the name, address, or telephone number of the company

body language—certain messages your body sends, communicated by expressions, gestures, and posture

budget—a plan for spending and saving money

C

civil rights—rights guaranteed to individuals by the U.S. Constitution, such as the right to equal treatment under the law

civil service worker—a person who holds a federal, state, or local government job

closed shop—a workplace where all workers must belong to the union and be included in the union contract

commission—pay that is a percentage of the amount of money a salesperson earns for a company

commute—to travel to and from a job

compromise—to give up part of your demands to come to an agreement

contract—a formal, written agreement between two or more people

controversy—a dispute or disagreement

co-pay—a part of the cost of a health care plan that workers are required to pay

cope—to successfully handle something that is difficult

cover letter—a type of application letter that aims

to persuade an employer to read an attached resume

credit union—an organization provided by a company or union that allows workers to borrow money at a lower interest rate and save money at a higher interest rate than other financial institutions

criterion/criteria—a standard, rule, or test by which something can be judged or measured

data—information, such as facts, numbers, or files

deductible—out-of-pocket medical expenses that a person must pay before medical insurance benefits begin

discriminate—to treat a person differently because of race, religion, national origin, ancestry, age, sex, or handicap

employee manual—a written guide that explains a company's rules and structure, information on fringe benefits, promotion procedures and more

Equal Employment Opportunity Commission (EEOC)—an agency that enforces federal civil rights laws

evaluate—to judge or rate the worth of something

exempt—free from a rule or obligation that applies to others; an employee who doesn't earn enough money to owe federal income tax may claim this status

expectation—something that is expected of a person

feedback—a person's response to another person's message

felony—a serious crime, such as murder or arson

flextime—a type of plan that allows workers to have flexible working hours, within certain limits

Form W-2—a wage and tax statement that an employee receives each January; shows how much money was earned during the past year and the amount deducted for taxes

Form W-4—a form that determines how much money will be deducted from a person's salary for federal and other income taxes; also called a withholding form

fringe benefit—payment to employees in a form other than money, such as health insurance or paid vacation time

grievance—a worker's complaint or problem with an employer that the union system attempts to resolve

gross pay—the pay a worker earns before any deductions are taken out

head of household—a claim allowed on a Form W-4 by a single parent who pays the household expenses

Health Maintenance Organization (HMO)—a group or association of doctors organized to provide low-cost medical care; works on the idea that making regular visits to the doctor prevents illnesses that result in expensive bills

hierarchy—a company's chain of command

hygiene—good health and cleanliness

income tax—a portion of a person's income that is paid to the federal and state governments

income tax return—a form used to figure out how much tax you should have paid for the past year

initiative—the desire to take on new responsibilities or challenges, or to start a task or project on one's own

interest—(1) a fee that banks or other institutions charge people for borrowing money; also, a fee paid to people for depositing money (2) an activity that you enjoy or something you like to talk or read about

interview—a meeting between an employer and a job applicant to determine an applicant's suitability for a job

itemize—to list income tax deductions by individual items

job description—a list of a job's responsibilities and everyday duties

job sharing—a situation in which two people share the same full-time job, and each person works part-time

labor union—an organization that bargains with employers on behalf of workers

latchkey—refers to school-age children who are home alone for several hours each day while parents are working

layoff—a temporary or permanent end to employment for workers that is usually done for economic reasons

long-term goal—a goal that may take some time to accomplish, such as taking a course at school

monitor—to watch or check a worker's performance

motivation—an influence that causes a person to act in a certain way

negotiate—to work out the terms of an agreement

net pay—the amount of pay a worker takes home after taxes and deductions have been taken out of gross pay; also called take-home pay

networking—the process of using personal contacts, such as friends, relatives, or acquaintances, to exchange information about jobs

objective—a statement on a resume that describes the kind of work a person is seeking

orientation day—a day when new employees learn about their new job and company; it's usually done before an employee's first working day

paystub—a written record that comes with a paycheck and shows the deductions from gross pay

performance review—an evaluation of a worker's performance; it's often an annual, formal meeting between an employer and employee regarding past job performance and future expectations

personality test—see *adjustment test*

personal trait—an individual quality of a person

personnel department—a department that is in charge of hiring for a company; also called department of human resources

potential—expressing possibility or capability

preference—something one prefers or likes better than something else

probationary period—the time during which a new employee's performance will be observed to determine if he or she is capable of doing the work

productivity—the amount of work an employee produces

promotion—an advance in position or rank within a company

qualification—knowledge, experience, or skill that makes a person suitable for a job

reference—a person, such as a past employer, teacher, or coach, who can tell an employer about a job applicant's character or work performance

referral—the action of directing someone elsewhere for information or aid

referral service—a place where a person can get a recommendation for a service needed, such as child care

resign—to quit a job

resume—a detailed, written summary of a job applicant's background and qualifications provided to an employer to determine an applicant's suitability

role—a part played by a person, such as worker, parent, or friend

salary—the amount of money a job pays

self-esteem—a good feeling a person has about himself or herself that helps in the achievement of goals

set priorities—to put goals in order of their importance

sexual harassment—improper advances or remarks of a sexual nature from a supervisor or co-worker

shift work—work period divisions that are common in industries operating 24 hours a day

shop steward—a member of a labor union who helps settle disputes between workers and management

short-term goal—a goal that may be reached right away

socialize—to be with a group of people and to interact with them

stress—mental and physical tension or strain

take-home pay—see *net pay*

talent—an aptitude that a person has for performing a certain skill

technical skill—a skill that is particular to a specific job, such as typing, using a cash register, or operating a forklift

time clock—a device that records the times when workers begin and finish working each day

trade-off—a giving up of some things you want in order to get other things you consider to be more desirable

traditional health care insurance—a type of insurance that protects people from major medical expenses and loss of income due to health-related problems; helps cover costs of doctors, hospitals, surgery, and medical emergencies

unemployment benefit—weekly pay for a worker who has been laid off or fired through no fault of his or her own

withholding form—see *Form W-4*

work permit—a document needed by people younger than the minimum working age in order to work in a business

work value—a feature of a job that is important to you, such as work environment, level of physical activity, or wages

ANSWER KEY

If answers are not provided, then answers will vary.

SECTION 1: TAKING STOCK OF YOURSELF

Word-Wise

Page 10

1. assets
2. interests
3. basic skills
4. work values

SECTION 2: WEIGHING YOUR OPTIONS

What's in an Ad?

Page 16

1. a job for a word processor
2. three years of word processing experience, general clerical skills, a minimum typing speed of 55 words per minute
3. no specific salary is listed
4. in downtown Chicago
5. by writing to Bob Clark
6. Bob Clark

Practice Using the Yellow Pages

Page 17

1. 608-609
2. 178
3. 344
4. 614
5. 610

What's in a Company Entry?

Page 18

1. plastics, fragrances, agricultural chemicals
2. 1,500
3. 83 Walnut Street, Powell, NY
4. $22,000,000
5. three

Word-Wise

Page 22

networking, blind ads, personnel department, interview

SECTION 3: TAKING THE NEXT STEPS

Word-Wise

Page 35

1. references
2. felony
3. resume
4. cover letter

Putting It to Work

Page 35

Answers should include any four of the following: your Social Security number; your visa number and expiration date; the names and addresses of schools you attended and dates when you attended them; the names, addresses, and telephone numbers of your last three employers; the starting and final pay for your last three jobs; the names, addresses, and telephone numbers of three references.

Getting the Facts

Page 35

1. Mr. Michael Williams, Personnel Director
2. a job as secretary

3. because she has educational training and clerical work experience

4. a position as a secretary

5. a receptionist/typist position at *The Smith Village News*

6. community college

SECTION 4: GETTING READY FOR INTERVIEWS

Try These Test Questions

Page 44

The answers are: b, c, and the following alphabetical list: debate, diner, dinner, dress, hardware, software, supplies, telephone, therapy

Word-Wise

Page 45

1. aptitude test

2. body language

3. potential

4. adjustment test or personality test

5. personal traits

Putting It to Work

Page 45-46

Any five of the following: find out about the company; find out about similar jobs; prepare to ask questions; practice answering questions; rehearse the interview; prepare to take tests; take care of other interview-related details.

SECTION 5: INTERVIEW DO'S AND DON'TS

Word-Wise

Page 55

discriminate, civil rights, Equal Employment Opportunity Commission, contract, evaluate

Putting It to Work

Page 56

Answers should mention any of the points discussed in Section 5.

SECTION 6: MAKING THE RIGHT CHOICE

Reading a Bus Schedule

Page 60

1. 8:20 A.M.

2. 30 minutes

3. 6:03 P.M.

4. find a different way to get to work

Figuring Out Pay

Page 62

Job #1: gross pay = $300
take-home pay = $240

Job #2: gross pay = $350
take-home pay = $280

Job #3: gross pay = $297.50
take-home pay = $238

Word-Wise

Page 66

1. flextime

2. gross pay

3. job sharing

4. net pay, take-home pay

5. trade-off

Putting It to Work

Page 66

Any five of the following: where the job is located; what hours you would work; how much money you would make; what benefits you would get; how much money you would spend to work; the working conditions; the chance for advancement.

SECTION 7: ADAPTING TO THE WORK WORLD

Filling Out a Timesheet

Page 72

Tuesday: In-8:30; Out-5:30

Wednesday: Sick

Thursday: In-9:30; Out-6:00

Friday: In-8:30; Out-5:30

Reading a Paystub

Page 77

Errors: Should have $10 deducted for the savings plan; should have $6.25 deducted for health insurance. Total deductions should be $103.25. Net pay should be $286.75.

Word-Wise

Page 79

1. allowance

2. hierarchy

3. head of household

4. adjustment period

5. job description

6. deductible

7. Form W-4

Putting It to Work

Page 79

Any five of the following: explain his responsibilities; explain employee policies and rules; answer any questions he has; introduce him to co-workers; give him a tour; show him how to fill out a Form W-4 and an insurance enrollment card; show him how to use a time card or timesheet; tell him when to expect his first paycheck.

Getting the Facts

Page 79

the Internal Revenue Service

SECTION 8: A BALANCING ACT

Planning a Budget

Page 88

Monthly Net Income	$1,145
Fixed Expenses	
Rent	$600
Transportation	$85
Electricity	$40
Telephone	$30
Food	$175
Variable Expenses	
Medical Costs	$40
Clothing	$50
Total	$1,020

1. $125

Word-Wise

Page 91

role, set priorities, short-term goals, long-term goals, budget, cope, stress

Putting It to Work

Page 91

Any five of the following: what hours care is available; what the cost is; whether parents can drop in any time; where the center is located; ratio of providers to children; providers' experience or training; parents' and children's reactions to providers; providers' reactions to children; whether place is large enough, safe, sanitary, cheerful; if there are interesting activities; if the children seem happy; what happens if children are sick; how emergencies, misbehavior, and mealtimes are handled.

SECTION 9: PROTECTING YOUR RIGHTS

What Form of Discrimination Is It?

Page 94

1. discrimination due to union activity

2. discrimination against a pregnant worker

3. gender discrimination

4. wage discrimination because of gender

5. age discrimination

Where to Find Help

Page 102

1. to OSHA

2. to the labor union

3. to any government or nongovernment organization mentioned

4. to your supervisor or employer

5. to the EEOC

6. to the ACLU or another civil rights organization

Word-Wise

Page 103

1. affirmative action

2. controversy

3. productivity

4. expectations

5. sexual harassment

Putting It to Work

Page 103

Any four of the following: to do a full day's work; to get to work on time; to do the work she's assigned without being told; to observe time limits for breaks; to work steadily until quitting time; to have a good reason when she's absent; to be capable, cooperative, honest, loyal, polite, and reliable.

SECTION 10: SUCCEEDING AT WORK

Expressing Yourself Positively

Page 106

These are suggested answers:

1. I will enjoy doing something different.
2. We both made that error, but we have learned from our mistake.
3. I would be glad to help him since we work as a team.
4. I'll help him, and maybe I can give him a hand getting organized.

Word-Wise

Page 113-114

1. probationary period
2. closed shop
3. criteria
4. grievances
5. shop steward

Putting It to Work

Page 114

Any five of the following: skill, quality of work, quantity of work, reliability, dependability, dealing with people, initiative.

Answers to the second part may include problems, questions, or any work-related subjects.

Getting the Facts

Page 114

1. the co-worker
2. your supervisor
3. your supervisor

4. someone in management or the human resources department
5. your supervisor
6. the shop steward
7. your supervisor

SECTION 11: MOVING UP THE LADDER

Word-Wise

Page 125-126

1. unemployment benefits
2. resign
3. self-esteem
4. motivation
5. ambition

Putting It to Work

Page 126

Any five of the following: carry out job tasks carefully and correctly; follow company rules; come in on time and work a full day and week; keep yourself and your work space neat and safe; show concern for the company and the product; grow with the job; volunteer to take on extra responsibility; get along with others at work.